THE SCRIPTURAL TEXT:
VERSES OF THE DOCTRINE,
WITH PARABLES

BDK English Tripiṭaka 10-II

THE SCRIPTURAL TEXT: VERSES OF THE DOCTRINE, WITH PARABLES

Translated from the Chinese of Fa-li and Fa-chü
(Taishō Volume 4, Number 211)

by

Charles Willemen

Numata Center
for Buddhist Translation and Research
1999

First Printing, 1999
ISBN: 1-886439-08-7
Library of Congress Catalog Card Number: 98-67121

Published by
Numata Center for Buddhist Translation and Research
2620 Warring Street
Berkeley, California 94704

Printed in the United States of America

A Message on the Publication of the English Tripiṭaka

The Buddhist canon is said to contain eighty-four thousand different teachings. I believe that this is because the Buddha's basic approach was to prescribe a different treatment for every spiritual ailment, much as a doctor prescribes a different medicine for every medical ailment. Thus his teachings were always appropriate for the particular suffering individual and for the time at which the teaching was given, and over the ages not one of his prescriptions has failed to relieve the suffering to which it was addressed.

Ever since the Buddha's Great Demise over twenty-five hundred years ago, his message of wisdom and compassion has spread throughout the world. Yet no one has ever attempted to translate the entire Buddhist canon into English throughout the history of Japan. It is my greatest wish to see this done and to make the translations available to the many English-speaking people who have never had the opportunity to learn about the Buddha's teachings.

Of course, it would be impossible to translate all of the Buddha's eighty-four thousand teachings in a few years. I have, therefore, had one hundred thirty-nine of the scriptural texts in the prodigious Taishō edition of the Chinese Buddhist canon selected for inclusion in the First Series of this translation project.

It is in the nature of this undertaking that the results are bound to be criticized. Nonetheless, I am convinced that unless someone takes it upon himself or herself to initiate this project, it will never be done. At the same time, I hope that an improved, revised edition will appear in the future.

It is most gratifying that, thanks to the efforts of more than a hundred Buddhist scholars from the East and the West, this monumental project has finally gotten off the ground. May the rays of the Wisdom of the Compassionate One reach each and every person in the world.

NUMATA Yehan
Founder of the English

August 7, 1991   Tripiṭaka Project

Editorial Foreword

In January 1982, Dr. NUMATA Yehan, the founder of the Bukkyō Dendō Kyōkai (Society for the Promotion of Buddhism), decided to begin the monumental task of translating the complete Taishō edition of the Chinese Tripiṭaka (Buddhist Canon) into the English language. Under his leadership, a special preparatory committee was organized in April 1982. By July of the same year, the Translation Committee of the English Tripiṭaka was officially convened.

The initial Committee consisted of the following members: HANAYAMA Shōyū (Chairperson); BANDŌ Shōjun; ISHIGAMI Zennō; KAMATA Shigeo; KANAOKA Shūyū; MAYEDA Sengaku; NARA Yasuaki; SAYEKI Shinkō; (late) SHIOIRI Ryōtatsu; TAMARU Noriyoshi; (late) TAMURA Kwansei; URYŪZU Ryūshin; and YUYAMA Akira. Assistant members of the Committee were as follows: KANAZAWA Atsushi; WATANABE Shōgo; Rolf Giebel of New Zealand; and Rudy Smet of Belgium.

After holding planning meetings on a monthly basis, the Committee selected one hundred thirty-nine texts for the First Series of translations, an estimated one hundred printed volumes in all. The texts selected are not necessarily limited to those originally written in India but also include works written or composed in China and Japan. While the publication of the First Series proceeds, the texts for the Second Series will be selected from among the remaining works; this process will continue until all the texts, in Japanese as well as in Chinese, have been published.

Frankly speaking, it will take perhaps one hundred years or more to accomplish the English translation of the complete Chinese and Japanese texts, for they consist of thousands of works. Nevertheless, as Dr. NUMATA wished, it is the sincere hope of the Committee that this project will continue unto completion, even after all its present members have passed away.

It must be mentioned here that the final object of this project is not academic fulfillment but the transmission of the teaching of the

Buddha to the whole world in order to create harmony and peace among mankind. To that end, the translators have been asked to minimize the use of explanatory notes of the kind which are indispensable in academic texts so that the attention of general readers will not be unduly distracted from the primary text. Also, a glossary of selected terms is appended to aid in understanding the text.

To my great regret, however, Dr. NUMATA passed away on May 5, 1994, at the age of 97, entrusting his son, Mr. NUMATA Toshihide, with the continuation and completion of the Translation Project. The Committee also lost its able and devoted Chairperson, Professor HANAYAMA Shōyū, on June 16, 1995, at the age of 63. After these severe blows, the Committee elected me, Vice-President of the Musashino Women's College, to be the Chair in October 1995. The Committee has renewed its determination to carry out the noble intention of Dr. NUMATA, under the leadership of Mr. NUMATA Toshihide.

The present members of the Committee are MAYEDA Sengaku (Chairperson), BANDŌ Shōjun, ISHIGAMI Zennō, ICHISHIMA Shōshin, KAMATA Shigeo, KANAOKA Shūyū, NARA Yasuaki, SAYEKI Shinkō, TAMARU Noriyoshi, URYŪZU Ryūshin, and YUYAMA Akira. Assistant members are WATANABE Shōgo and UEDA Noboro.

The Numata Center for Buddhist Translation and Research was established in November 1984, in Berkeley, California, U.S.A., to assist in the publication of the BDK English Tripiṭaka First Series. In December 1991, the Publication Committee was organized at the Numata Center, with Professor Philip Yampolsky as the Chairperson. To our sorrow, Professor Yampolsky passed away in July 1996, but thankfully Dr. Kenneth Inada is continuing the work as Chairperson. This text is the seventeenth volume to be published and distributed by the Numata Center. All of the remaining texts will be published under the supervision of this Committee, in close cooperation with the Translation Committee in Tokyo.

MAYEDA Sengaku
Chairperson
Translation Committee of
the BDK English Tripiṭaka

June 10, 1999

Publisher's Foreword

The Publication Committee works in close cooperation with the Editorial Committee of the BDK English Tripiṭaka in Tokyo, Japan. Since December 1991, it has operated from the Numata Center for Buddhist Translation and Research in Berkeley, California. Its principal mission is to oversee and facilitate the publication in English of selected texts from the one hundred-volume Taishō Edition of the Chinese Tripiṭaka, along with a few major influential Japanese Buddhist texts not in the Tripiṭaka. The list of selected texts is conveniently appended at the end of each volume. In the text itself, the Taishō Edition page and column designations are provided in the margins.

The Committee is committed to the task of publishing clear, readable English texts. It honors the deep faith, spirit, and concern of the late Reverend Doctor NUMATA Yehan to disseminate Buddhist teachings throughout the world.

In July 1996, the Committee unfortunately lost its valued Chairperson, Dr. Philip Yampolsky, who was a stalwart leader, trusted friend, and esteemed colleague. We follow in his shadow. In February 1997, I was appointed to guide the Committee in his place.

The Committee is charged with the normal duties of a publishing firm—general editing, formatting, copyediting, proofreading, indexing, and checking linguistic fidelity. The Committee members are Diane Ames, Eisho Nasu, Charles Niimi, Koh Nishiike, and the president and director of the Numata Center, Reverend Kiyoshi S. Yamashita.

We are now extremely happy to publish the Chinese version of the *Dhammapada* with very apt and illuminating parables and lengthy commentaries on the verses. A few of the verses coincide with the Pali version. Overall, however, it reveals the Chinese way of thinking and the consequent brand of Buddhism in the making.

The reader is cautioned that there are remarks expressing attitudes about women which can be seen as inaccurate and insulting. This translation should be read in historical context.

Kenneth K. Inada
Chairperson
June 10, 1999   Publication Committee

Contents

A List of the Volumes of the BDK English Tripiṭaka   (First Series)

Translator's Introduction

The scriptural text called *Fa-chü* (Verses of the Doctrine, *Dhammapada*) *p'i-yü* (Parables, *Avadāna*), *ching* (sutra) T. IV 211, pp. 575–609, belongs to the so-called *Dhammapada* literature.

The *Dhammapada*

The Theravāda *Dhammapada,* a text of four hundred twenty-three stanzas in twenty-six chapters, is probably the most widely translated Buddhist text since V. Fausböll translated it into Latin in 1855. Suffice it here to refer to the widely used translation by S. Radhakrishnan, *The Dhammapada,* Oxford University Press, Madras, 1966 (first Indian printing). The text presents Buddhist ethics in a popular way. There is also an *Aṭṭhakathā,* a commentary, attributed to Buddhaghosa (fl. ca. 400 C.E.). This text essentially tells us the stories pertaining to the stanzas. The whole was translated into English by E. W. Burlingame, *Buddhist Legends,* London 1969, in three volumes, published by the Pāli Text Society.

The Pāli *Dhammapada* exists in more than one Chinese version. Best known is the *Fa-chü (Dhammapada) ching,* T. 210. The core of the text is the twenty-six chapters of the Pāli *Dhammapada,* but it contains thirteen additional chapters. In its preface, Wei-ch'i-nan (Vighna) is mentioned as the translator. He probably translated the text in or shortly after 224 C.E. The Indo-Scythian *upāsaka* Chih Ch'ien, working in Chien-yeh, very probably revised this translation and enlarged it, adding the thirteen chapters. It is this text and his preface that we read as T. 210, in which the twenty-six chapters of the *Dhammapada* are divided into two parts

1

of thirteen chapters each. With the exception of the *Sakkāravagga*, the thirteen chapters that do not appear in the *Dhammapada* have been placed either before or after the central core of the text. These thirteen chapters seem to derive to a great extent from an *Udānavarga*, as indicated by titles such as *anicca, suta, saddhā, sīla, sati, vācā, sakkāra,* and *nibbāna*. Besides, the additional chapters opening the text correspond to the *Udānavarga*, while those added at the end hardly have any such correspondence. These chapters are taken not from an *Udānavarga*, but from other texts such as the *Suttanipāta*. As yet, there is no translation of the complete Chinese text in a European language.

The *Fa-chü p'i-yü ching*

This text was written by the two *śramaṇa*s Fa-li and Fa-chü, at the time of Emperor Hui of the Western Chin (290–306 C.E.). The authors selected stanzas from the earlier translation, i.e., from the *Fa-chü ching,* adding a commentary, *p'i-yü (avadāna)*, and parables. They did not translate any particular Indian text, since the *Fa-chü ching*, even though its core is the Pāli *Dhammapada,* also consists of translations from other texts, among them the *Udānavarga*. The commentary added by Fa-li and Fa-chü to selected stanzas of this *Fa-chü ching* is probably based on Indian texts. The entire *Fa-chü p'i-yü ching* is here for the first time translated into English. Its doctrinal affiliation is still Theravāda. The original Indian language certainly was not Sanskrit. Although it may have been composed in Pāli, there is no connection whatsoever with Buddhaghosa's alleged *Aṭṭhakathā*.

The *Udānavarga*

It must be noted that there are two more Chinese texts in the *Dhammapada* literature. One is called the *Ch'u-yao (Udāna) ching,* T. 212, translated from the Sanskrit in 399 C.E. by the Indian Saṃghabhadra and by Chu Fo-nien, a *śramaṇa* of Indian origin from Liang-chou. The concept of this text is the same as that of the Pāli *Udāna*. It records the circumstances under which a stanza was pronounced. The stanzas of its thirty-three chapters form the *Udānavarga* as we know it. The other text is called *Fa-chi-yao-sung (Udānavarga) ching,* T. 213, translated from the Sanskrit in 985 C.E. by the Indian monk T'ien-hsi-tsai (Deva) (śāntika?). This text is the Chinese *Udānavarga.* The whole text was translated into English by C. Willemen, *The Chinese Udānavarga: A Collection of Important Odes of the Law,* Brussels, 1978. The *Udāna* and the *Udānavarga* belong to the Sarvāstivāda school. The *Udānavarga* is the *Dharmapada* of the Sarvāstivādins. The Chinese translators considered both the *Udāna* and the *Udānavarga* to be of the same nature as the *Fa-chü ching,* as the translation of the corresponding stanzas proves.

THE SCRIPTURAL TEXT:
VERSES OF THE DOCTRINE,
WITH PARABLES

Translated by the ascetics (*śramaṇa*s)

Fa-chü and Fa-li

during the Western Chin Dynasty

Volume One

Chapter I

Impermanence

At one time, the five qualities of Śakra, Lord of the Gods, left him. 575b
He knew that his life would end and that he would descend to be
born in the world, conceived in the womb of an ass in a pottery.
What do they say are the five qualities? First, the light about the
person is extinguished. Second, the flowers above the head wither.
Third, one wants to leave one's seat. Fourth, the perspiration under the armpits is strong-smelling. Fifth, defilement sticks to the
body. Because of these five things he knew that his merit had
ended, and he felt utterly dejected. He recalled that only the
Buddha might save people from their hardship in the three realms,
so he hastened to where the Buddha dwelled. At that time the
Buddha was sitting in meditation in a cave on Mount Gṛdhrakūṭa,
having entered the *samādhi* of universal rescue. When the Lord
of the Gods saw the Buddha, he kowtowed, did obeisance, and
prostrated himself and earnestly took the triple refuge: in the
Buddha, in his Doctrine (Dharma), and in his Community
(Sangha). Before he could stand up, his life suddenly ended. He
then arrived in a pottery, as the young in the belly of a she-ass.
The ass then pulled herself loose and ran around in the pottery,
breaking the earthenware. Her owner beat her and as a result
injured her pregnant womb. Śakra's spirit immediately returned
to his old body. Endowed anew with the five qualities, he was the

7

575c   Lord of the Gods again. The Buddha awoke from his *samādhi* and he said in praise: "Excellent it is, Lord of the Gods, when you can take refuge in the Three Honorable Things (the Buddha, Dharma, and Sangha) when you are about to die. When the retribution for your evil is over, you will not suffer again." Then the World-honored One spoke the stanzas:

> 1. Formations are impermanent, that is to say, it is their nature to arise and to pass away. When they have come into being, they suddenly pass away. Their allayment means happiness.

> 2. When for instance a potter makes earthenware with diluted earth, it will all break. It is the same with a man's life.

When Lord Śakra heard the stanzas, he knew that impermanence was inevitable. He recognized that evil and merit change, he understood that arising and passing away are fundamental, and he followed the path of tranquility. He acknowledged this with joy and attained the path of the stream-enterer (*srotaāpanna*).

The Buddha once was in a pure abode in the land of Śrāvastī and expounded the Doctrine to gods, men, dragons, and demons. The queen mother of Prasenajit, the ruler of the land, was more than ninety years old then, and she suddenly fell seriously ill. Medicinal herbs did not make her better, and so she died. The king and the ministers of the land held a funeral according to the rules. They moved her spirit to a grave. When the funeral was over, they passed by the Buddha on their way back. They took off their garments, removed their stockings, and did a deep obeisance in front of the Buddha. The Buddha told them to sit down, and he asked them: "The clothes are coarse where you come from, O King, and they look different. Why this behavior?" The king kowtowed and said: "The queen mother of the land was more than ninety years old when she recently fell seriously ill. She soon passed away. We have escorted her spirit and her coffin to her grave. We are

8

just now on our way back, and while passing by we visit you, O Noble Reverend." The Buddha informed the king: "From of old to this day there have been four great fears: to be born and grow old and wither; to lose one's spiritual brightness through illness; to lose the spirit after death; and to be separated from one's loved ones. These are said to be the four. They do not give man any fixed time. As all things are impermanent, it is difficult to achieve permanence. Everything passes in a day. Man's life is like that. As the five rivers ceaselessly flow day and night, just so is the rapid passing of man's life." Thereupon the World-honored One spoke the stanza:

> 3. As a river that swiftly flows and, once gone, will not
> return, so is man's life. Those who are gone do not return.

The Buddha informed the great king that this applies to the whole world. "None stays long. All must die and none escapes death. The kings of the past, the Buddhas and the saints, the seers with the five superknowledges, they have all gone too. None could stay. It is useless to grieve for any harm that befalls the body. If one mourns the deceased as a pious son, one performs merits and one does what is meritorious. Being presented with this, one keeps returning. One is followed by the merits as provisions [follow] someone on a long journey." When the Buddha had said this, the king and his ministers all rejoiced. They forgot their sorrow and gave up suffering. All who had come attained the Path.

Once the Buddha was in the Veṇuvana (Bamboo Grove) in Rājagṛha. He entered the city with his disciples. After he had expounded the Doctrine upon request, he left the city in the afternoon.   576a
On his way, he met someone driving a big herd of well-fed cows back to the city. Bobbing up and down and twisting, they bumped into each other. Thereupon the World-honored One spoke the stanzas:

> 4. When, for instance, a cowherd with his staff takes his
> cattle to the pasture to feed them, that would be like old
> age-death. They also sustain life.

5. It is not just well-born men and women, but hundreds and thousands of people who amass possessions; yet all will perish.

6. For all who have been born, their lives are besieged night and day. The termination of life is like a well that becomes dry.

When the Buddha arrived in the Bamboo Garden, he washed his feet, stepped back, and sat down. Ānanda came forward, kowtowed, and asked: "O World-honored One, a while ago you expounded on these three stanzas along the way. I still do not know their meaning. Would you please explain them to me?" The Buddha informed Ānanda: "Did you see a man driving a herd of cattle?" "Yes, I saw him." The Buddha informed Ānanda: "The herd of this butcher used to number a thousand head. Every day the butcher sent someone out of the city to look for fine water and grass, feeding them so that they would become fat and tall. Every day he would pick out the fat ones, lead them away, and have them killed. After he had killed more than half of them, the remaining ones still did not take any notice. They just kept bumping into each other, bobbed up and down, and mooed. Because I felt pity for their ignorance, I spoke the stanzas." The Buddha said to Ānanda: "But why only these cattle? The same applies to people. Counting on their selves, they do not know about impermanence. They nourish themselves in a gluttonous way with the five objects of desire. Cheerfully and utterly gratified, they then destroy each other. Because of impermanence, retribution for their past is suddenly upon them when they do not expect it. Because they dwell in ignorance, they are not aware of this. Is this any different?" Among those who were sitting there at the time, there were two hundred monks (*bhikṣus*) who coveted honors. Hearing the Doctrine and having encouraged themselves, they achieved the six superknowledges and became arhats. All those who were seated there felt compassion and joy, and they did obeisance to the Buddha.

Once the Buddha was in Śrāvastī, in the Anāthapiṇḍada Grove in the Jetavana, expounding the Doctrine to his disciples. The daughter of a brahman was present. She was fourteen or fifteen years old, beautiful and clever of speech. Her father loved her very much. She suddenly fell seriously ill and died immediately. It was as though there were ripe wheat in the field that was consumed by fire. Upon experiencing this sorrow and grief, the brahman lost his senses and was confused. He could not understand and felt like a fool. He heard people say that the Buddha was a great sage, and that as a teacher of gods and men he expounded the path of the scriptural texts, making them forget their sorrow and doing away with their suffering. Thereupon the brahman went to the Buddha. He did obeisance, knelt down, and said to the Buddha: "Up to now my children have been few. I just had one daughter. My love for her made me forget my sorrow, but she suddenly fell seriously ill. She abandoned me and died. I am in low spirits, and I cannot overcome my feelings. Please, World-honored One, have pity on me and instruct me! Dispel the fetters of my sorrow!" The Buddha informed the brahman thusly: "There are four things in 576b the world that cannot last long. What are these four? (1) What is constant will certainly be impermanent; (2) wealth will certainly become poverty; (3) meeting will certainly become separation; (4) the strong will certainly die." Thereupon the World-honored One spoke the stanza:

> 7. All things constant will end. That which is high will
> nevertheless come down. Any coming together implies
> separation. The living will die.

When the brahman heard the stanza, his mind suddenly opened up and he wished to become a monk. As his beard and his hair fell off of themselves, he became a monk. Again reflecting upon the nature of impermanence, he entered the path of an arhat.

Once the Buddha was on Mount Gṛdhrakūṭa in Rājagṛha. At that time there was a luscious lady in the city. She was called Padmā.

Her beauty was unparalleled in the land. High officials and young people all sought her company and held her in high esteem. A wholesome thought then arose of itself in Padmā. She wanted to abandon her worldly affairs and become a nun (*bhikṣuṇī*). So she went to the mountain, to where the Buddha was. Before she reached the halfway point, she came to a spring with flowing water. When Padmā drank some water and washed her hands, she saw the image of her face. Her complexion was dazzling and her hair was dark blue. Her appearance was well proportioned and beautiful beyond compare. She felt regret and said: "When one is born into this world with such an appearance, why throw oneself away and become an ascetic? I should follow the times and enjoy my personal passion!" With this in mind, she returned. But the Buddha knew that Padmā should be saved. He changed into a woman, a paragon of beauty, excelling even Padmā tens of thousands of times. Seeking Padmā out, she came toward her. Padmā saw her, and she felt deep affection and respect. So she asked the transformed person where she came from, where her husband and children, her father and brothers all were, whether at home or away, and why she was walking all alone, without any attendants. The transformed person replied: "I come from town and I want to return home. Although I do not know you, it would be nice to return together. Shall we both rest and talk at the spring?" Padmā agreed, and they both went back to the spring together. When they had spoken at length about what was on their minds, the transformed person became sleepy. She lay her head down in Padmā's lap and fell asleep. After a while her life suddenly ended. She became swollen and putrid. Her belly burst and worms came out. Her teeth fell out and hair dropped. Her body's limbs fell off. When Padmā saw this, she was very disturbed. "Why is this lovely person all of a sudden impermanent? If this is the case even for this person, how could I be preserved for a long time? I must go to the Buddha and zealously apply myself to the Path!" She then went to the Buddha and prostrated herself. Having done obeisance, she explained everything she had seen to the Buddha. The Buddha informed Padmā: "Man has four things on which he cannot depend. Which four? One: youthful vigor; it will eventually turn to old age. Two: strong health; it will eventually turn to death. Three: the six relatives; although they bring pleasure, they will eventually be gone. Four: riches; when they are accumulated, they will eventually be scattered." Thereupon the World-honored One spoke these stanzas: 576c

> 8. When one is old, beauty fades away. The healthy fall ill and are ruined. The body collapses, putrefied. That is the way life ends.

> 9. What is the use of this body, something constantly dripping and smelly! It is worn out by illness and suffers the calamities of old age-death.

> 10. When one indulges in lust and is licentious, evil increases. One does not see the changes, but life is impermanent.

> 11. One cannot depend on a son, or a father, or a brother. Oppressed by death, one does not have any relative on whom to rely.

When Padmā heard the Doctrine, she was happy and full of understanding. She saw the body as a transformation. Life does not remain the same. Indeed, having the quality of the Path, nirvana is eternal happiness. So she said to the Buddha that she wanted to become a nun. The Buddha said: "Excellent!" Her hair fell off and she became a nun. She cultivated right contemplation and became an arhat. When all who were sitting there had heard the Buddha's explanation, there was none who was not happy.

Once the Buddha was in the city of Rājagṛha, expounding the Doctrine in the Veṇuvana (Bamboo Grove). There were brahmans present, four brothers who each had achieved five superknowledges. Seven days later, each one's life would end. They talked it over among themselves and said: "There is nothing we cannot do with the power of our five superknowledges: reversing heaven and earth, stopping the sun and moon, moving mountains, and stopping currents. How can we not escape from this retribution of death?" One said: "I shall enter the ocean. Invisible from above and not on the bottom underneath, I shall stay right in the middle. How could the murderous demon of impermanence know my whereabouts?" Another said: "I shall enter Mount Sumeru and close its surface again [over me] so that I shall never be visible. How could the murderous demon of impermanence know my whereabouts?" Another said: "I shall soar lightly and hide in the sky. How would the murderous demon of impermanence know my whereabouts?" Another said: "I shall conceal myself in a large marketplace. When the murderous demon of impermanence rushes to take someone, why would he necessarily look for me?" When the four men had talked about it, they went to take leave of the king: "We calculate that we have seven days left to live. We want to flee for our lives now, and we hope we will be able to escape. After our return we shall personally visit you. Please, may you advance in virtue!"

Thereupon they parted and each went to his own place. When the period of seven days was over, the life of each one ended, like fruit that is ripe and falls. The market supervisor informed the king that there was a brahman who had suddenly died in the market. The king understood and said: "The four men were going to escape from their retribution. One is already dead. How could the remaining three be exempt!" The king then had his chariot made ready, and he drove to where the Buddha was. He did obeisance, stepped back, and sat down. He informed the Buddha: "Recently there were brahmans, four brothers, who each had achieved the five superknowledges. They knew their lives would end, and

577a they were all going to escape death. I wonder if they can still avoid it?" The Buddha said to the great king that human beings have four things from which they cannot escape. What are the four? First: being in an intermediate state one cannot but experience birth. Second: being born one cannot but experience old age. Third: having grown old one cannot but experience illness. Fourth: being

14

ill one cannot but experience death. Thereupon the World-honored One spoke the stanzas:

> 12. Neither in the air nor in the sea, nor in the depths of a mountain cave, is there a place on earth where one might escape and not experience death.

> 13. It is my duty; this is my task; I shall act so that I shall bring about what is right! People fret about this and they go through the sorrows of old age and death.

> 14. Knowing this, one can appease oneself, thus seeing the end of birth. O monks, reject Māra's soldiers and be delivered from the birth and death cycle!

When the king heard the Buddha's words, he said in admiration: "Excellent! This is truly in accord with your teaching, O Reverend! The four men were going to escape from their retribution, but one has already died. The same will happen to the others, sharing their fate!" Among the ministers and officials there was none who did not have faith.

Chapter II

Training

Once the Buddha was in the land of Śrāvastī, in the pure abode of the Jetavana. The Buddha informed the monks: "Diligently cultivate the Path and avoid the rise of any hindrance! When your mind is clear and your spirit is concentrated, you can escape any suffering." There was a monk whose determination was not fully clear. Having eaten his fill he went to his room, closed the door, and quietly went to sleep. Fond of his own self and light in mind, he could not contemplate impermanence. Because he was dull and lazy, day or night meant nothing to him anymore. After seven days his life would surely end. The Buddha had pity on him. He feared that he would fall into an evil path. So he entered the monk's room, snapped his fingers to wake him up, and said:

1. Get up! Why are you sleeping? You gadfly, conch, oyster, or worm, you are covered with impurity. In your delusion you assume you are a person.

2. You are covered with sores and your mind is afflicted with ailments. Meeting with any hardship, all you do is resort to sleep.

3. Reflect and do not be negligent! To be a human being, apply yourself to a path of benevolence! As a result you will not know sorrow. Always keep it in mind to extinguish your intentions!

4. He who has correct views and applies himself to strengthen them stands out brightly in the world. The merit he produces is thousandfold, and he will never fall into an evil path.

When the monk heard the stanzas, he immediately woke up, startled. Seeing that the Buddha himself was admonishing him, his respect increased and he gasped with fright. So he rose, kowtowed, and did obeisance to the Buddha. The Buddha said to the monk: "Would it be that you know your former lives?" The monk answered: "I am beset by hindrances. I really do not know." The Buddha said to the monk: "Once in the time of the Buddha Vipaśyin, you went forth, but you coveted personal honors and you were not mindful of the disciplinary prescriptions in the scriptural texts. Having eaten to the full you withdrew to sleep, not mindful of impermanence. Your life ended and you were reborn among gadflies. You accumulated fifty thousand years and your life ended. You later became a conch and an oyster, and a worm in a tree, for fifty thousand years each. These four kinds of insects live in lasting obscurity. They are egoistic and long for life. They like to stay in seclusion. Obscurity is their home, and they do not see any light. Waking up follows after a sleeping time of a hundred years. You were bound in the net of evil and did not seek that which was essential to leave it. Only now has your evil come to an end and have you become an ascetic. Why do you not get enough of sleeping?" Thereupon the monk again heard about his previous causality, and he felt mortified and reproved himself. The clouds of the five hindrances dissipated, and he immediately attained arhatship.

577b (margin)

Once the Buddha was in the land of Śrāvastī, in the Anāthapiṇḍada Grove in the Jetavana, together with gods and men, expounding the Doctrine with the four classes (monks, nuns, laymen, and laywomen). Among them was a young monk, a foolish man. His disposition was rude and he had not yet understood the essentials of the Path. His affections were strong and he aspired after lust. His virility was potent and he could not restrain himself. He considered this to be the vexation that made it impossible for him to be saved. While meditating he thought, "It is my penis. If I cut it off, I can be pure and be able to obtain the Path." So he went to the house of a *dānapati* (liberal donor) and borrowed a hatchet from him. He returned to his quarters, shut the door, and took off his clothes. He sat down upon a wooden board with the intention of chopping off his penis. [He thought:] "Just because of this penis I am made to suffer, passing through the birth and death cycle for countless eons. The three depraved destinations and the six creatures all result from lust. If I do not cut this off, I shall not have any way of obtaining the Path." The Buddha knew what was on his mind and how foolish he was. [He thought:] "The Path results from restraining the thoughts. Thoughts are the foundation. Ignorant of his mortality he hurts himself. He will fall into evil and experience suffering for a long time." Thereupon the World-honored One entered the monk's quarters and asked him: "What are you trying to do! Put down the hatchet and get dressed!" The monk greeted the Buddha and stated: "I have been applying myself to the Path for a long time, but I do not understand the way of the Doctrine yet. Every time I sit in meditation I am steeped in desire just when I am about to obtain the Path. My virility is so potent that I am confused and remain in darkness. Unaware of heaven and earth, I clearly blame myself and think it all is the result of this penis. That is why I borrowed a hatchet, wanting to do away with it." The Buddha informed the monk: "How foolish you are! You do not understand the principle. If one wants to seek the Path, one must first eliminate one's foolishness and then control one's thoughts! Thoughts are the basis of good and evil. If you want to do away with your roots, you must first of all control your thoughts. When your thoughts are calmed and your mind clear, you will obtain the Path." Thereupon the World-honored One spoke the stanza:

> 5. If he applies himself first to relinquish the thought of his mother, if he guides the ruler's two ministers, and if he gives up all attendants, he is a superior man of the Path.

577c

The Buddha informed the monk: "Delusion is the basis of the twelve causes (*nidāna*s). Delusion is the source of all evil. Knowledge should be the basis of all actions! Only when you have first eliminated delusion will your mind be settled." After the Buddha had said this, the monk was ashamed, and so he reproved himself and said: "Ever since I was misled by my foolishness, I have never understood the old scriptures, so that I am like this! Your explanation just now, O Buddha, is truly wonderful!" He internally considered right concentration and breathing while counting (*ānāpāna*). Guarding his mind and restraining his thoughts, he subdued his affections and shut out all desire, and so his mind was settled. In the presence of the Buddha he attained arhatship.

Once the Buddha was on Mount Gṛdhrakūṭa in the land of Rājagṛha, explaining the doctrine of immortality to gods and men, to the king and his high officials. There was one monk who was willful and reckless. The Buddha knew how he was and sent him to a valley of spirits in the mountains. He had him sit down under a tree to count his breaths and practice concentration. [He said:] "Knowing the length and brevity of the breaths, *ānāpāna* (breathing exercise) guards the mind. Having removed any longing and extinguished suffering, one may obtain nirvana." When the monk had received the instructions, he went to the valley. He sat up straight and concentrated his mind, but he only heard the voices of the spirits in the mountains. He did not see their likenesses. There were only sounds and he gasped with fright. He was so terrified that he could not calm himself. He wanted to return [home] regretfully, but he thought to himself: "The house I lived in was that of a very wealthy family. Yet I insisted on going forth, to become a monk, to apply myself to the Path, and to see the place of happiness for myself. Neither have I a companion nor is there any practitioner deep in the spirit mountains. There are only demons who frequently come to frighten people." While he was thinking in this way and before he went back, the World-honored One went to his side. He sat down under a tree and asked him: "You are alone here. Aren't you afraid?" The monk kowtowed and said: "I have never been in the mountains before. I was really

worried here." After a while there was a wild elephant king who
came by. He lay down against a tree, happy all by himself, [think-
ing:] "How pleasant to be away from the other elephants!" The
Buddha knew what was on the elephant's mind, and he said to the
monk: "Would you know where this elephant comes from?" He
replied: "I do not know." The Buddha informed the monk: "The
size of this elephant's herd is more than five hundred head. Wearied by the small elephants, he left them and came here. Lying
down against a tree, he is thinking how pleasing it is to have left
the prison of love. An elephant may be an animal, but he thinks
about a solitary abode. How much more must you leave your family and seek salvation! But in fact, because of your loneliness, you
seek companionship! One is often hurt by foolish companions.
One who stays alone has no antagonists and is free from scheming. It is better to develop the Path all alone. There is no need for
a foolish companion." Thereupon the World-honored One spoke
the stanzas:

> 6. If one does not have a companion in learning, nor a
> good friend, one had better safeguard one's own good
> conduct rather than associate with a fool!   578a

> 7. Finding joy in the precepts and training in [righteous]
> living, why would one need the doings of a companion? Be
> virtuous on your own and free from grief, like the elephant
> in the open wilderness.

When the Buddha expounded this, the monk understood. He internally considered the noble teaching and became an arhat. The
spirits in the valley all understood too, and became the Buddha's
disciples. They accepted the precepts and did not frighten people
any more. The Buddha returned to the pure abode together with
the monks.

Once the Buddha was in the land of Śrāvastī, in the pure abode of
the Jetavana, expounding the scriptural Doctrine to gods and men.
In the land of Rājagṛha there were two novice monks who wanted

to meet the Buddha. Between the two countries, however, there was a desert without any people. At that time, there was a drought and the springs were dry. The two monks were starving and thirsty, gasping feverishly. In an old spring they found plenty of water, but tiny insects made it impossible for them to drink it. The two said to each other: "We came from afar expressly to see the Buddha. We did not imagine that we would die here today." One said: "Let us drink some water to save our lives. When we go and see the Buddha, how will he know the circumstances?" The other responded: "Among the Buddha's profound precepts, compassion is the most important. If one destroys one's life to stay alive, it is useless to meet the Buddha. However, one should keep the precepts and die rather than violate the precepts and live." So the first one stood up, quickly drank with utmost eagerness, and then continued on his way. The other one did not drink and consequently brought about his own death, but he was immediately reborn in the Trāyastriṃśa heaven. After consideration and self-examination, he knew that in his previous life he had kept and not violated the precepts. "As I am reborn here now, truly a meritorious retribution is not far off!" [he thought]. Holding fragrant flowers, he descended to the Buddha. He greeted the Buddha, stepped back, and stood aside. The one who had drunk some water arrived a few days later, exhausted by the journey. He saw that the Buddha's spiritual qualities were utterly venerable and imposing. He kowtowed, and having greeted him he stated with tears in his eyes: "My one companion has died yonder. I am sad that he did not make it. I want you, O Buddha, to know that." The Buddha said: "I already know." The Buddha pointed with his finger and said, "Well, this heavenly person was your companion. He kept the precepts intact, was reborn in heaven, and arrived here first!" Thereupon the World-honored One bared his breast and showed it to him. [He said:] "You see my appearance, but you do not keep my precepts. Even though you may say that you see me, I do not see you. That person who has followed the precepts of the scriptures, though ten thousand miles away from me, is here before my eyes."

Thereupon the World-honored One spoke the stanzas:

> 8. When one is learned in one's training, and when he keeps the precepts and does not break them, he is praised in both worlds. His wishes will be fulfilled.

> 9. When one has little learning in one's training, and does not completely keep the precepts, he experiences suffering in both worlds. His wishes will not be fulfilled.

> 10. He who is in training has two things: he is always close to the learned and, dwelling in the truth, he understands the meaningful. Even though he may be in trouble, he does not go astray.

578b

Then, when the monk heard the stanzas, he felt mortified and kowtowed. He repented his error and silently thought about what he had done. When the heavenly person heard the stanzas, his mind was pleased and he obtained the eye of the Doctrine. There was none in the crowd of gods and men who did not follow [the instructions].

Chapter III

The Very Learned

Once there was a poor family in the land of Śrāvastī. Husband and wife were stingy and they did not believe in the virtue of the Path. The Buddha felt pity for their foolishness. Looking like a poor ascetic, he went to their gate to beg for food. The husband was not in at the time, but his wife scolded him beyond reason. The ascetic said to her: "I am a man of the Path and I live on alms. You do not have to scold me; I am just looking forward to some food!" The master's wife said: "If you stood there dying, you still would not get any food! How much less so if you want my food now that you are healthy. You are just wasting my time. You had better go away at once!" The ascetic then kept standing in front of her. He stared, gave his last breath, and appeared to be dead. His body was swollen and out of his nose and mouth came worms. His belly burst and his bowels were in a state of decomposition and impurities flowed forth. When the wife saw him, she was alarmed and lost her voice. She ran away and left him. Thereupon the man of the Path was suddenly gone. Some miles away from her home, she sat down underneath a tree to rest. The husband met his wife while he was on his way back home, and he wondered why she was afraid. The wife told him that there was this ascetic whose appearance terrified her. Upon seeing him she was so afraid. The husband became angry and asked where the ascetic might be. His wife said: "He is gone, but I think he is not yet far away." The husband took his bow and girded on his sword. Looking for tracks, he went after the ascetic. Flexing his bow and with drawn sword, he ran straight ahead with the intention of chopping down the man of the Path. The man of the Path then magically created a wall of lapis lazuli and surrounded himself with it. The husband ran several times along the wall, but could not get through. So he asked the man of the Path why he did not open the gate. The man of the Path replied: "If you want me to open the gate, throw away your bow and sword!" The husband thought to himself: "I must follow his words. But when I am inside, I shall beat him up." He then threw away his bow and sword, but the gate still did not open. He further said to the man of the Path: "I have thrown away my bow and sword. Why doesn't the gate open?" The man of the Path said: "I want you to throw away the bow and sword stemming from the evil intentions in your mind! I do not mean the bow and sword physically in your hands!" Thereupon the man was startled and very confused. [He thought:] "The man of the Path is a supernaturally noble one who knows my thoughts." He immediately kowtowed and repented his mistake. He explained to the man of the Path: "I have a wicked wife who does not recognize a man of truth. She is the instigator of my wickedness. Please have compassion and do not abandon us now! I would like you to exhort her to train in the Path." So he stood up and went back to his wife, who asked him: "Where is the ascetic?" Her husband gave a full explanation of his miraculous power and replied, "He is back there now. You should reform yourself by extinguishing your evil." When the husband and wife reached the man of the Path, they profoundly repented of their sensual errors and desired to be his disciples. They knelt and asked the man of the Path: "Your supernatural power and noble intelligence are immense! You have a wall of lapis lazuli, solid and hard to cross. Your resolve is clear and your mind is firm. You are forever free from sorrow. Which qualities of the Path did you practice to bring about such wondrous excellence?" The man of the Path answered: "My extensive learning is insatiable and I unremittingly follow the Doctrine. Zeal, moral conduct, patience, and heedfulness: because of these one opens the Path and brings about nirvana." Thereupon the man of the Path spoke the stanzas:

578c

26

1. Because one firmly maintains extensive learning and pursues the Dharma, one becomes like a hard wall; one's zeal then does not break down. At that point morality and wisdom are accomplished.

2. Great learning makes one's resolve clear. As it is clear, wisdom increases. As wisdom sets in, one widely understands the essence of things. Perceiving the essences, one is happy following the Dharma.

3. Great learning can remove sorrow, and, with concentration, promote joyfulness. Explaining the law of immortality well, one brings about the gaining of nirvana.

4. Learning is to know the Dharma. It dispels doubt and sees what is right. He who as a result of his learning rejects what is improper arrives at the state of immortality.

When the man of the Path had spoken the stanzas, he showed the bright appearance of the Buddha. His ample radiance was glorious, illuminating heaven and earth. The husband and wife were frightened and their spirits were terrified. They abandoned their evils and cleansed their thoughts, beating their heads on the ground. They did away with the manifold evils and obtained the path of the stream-enterer.

Once the Buddha was in the pure abode of Ghoṣila in Kauśāmbī, together with the four classes, explaining the great Dharma. There was a brahman, a man of the Path, whose knowledge was extensive. He was thoroughly versed in the scriptural texts and, seemingly, there was nothing he was not versed in. He was haughty and praised himself as unequaled in the world. He went looking for someone to debate with, but no one dared to comply. One day he was walking in the marketplace carrying a torch, and someone asked him: "Why are you walking with a torch in your hand in the daytime?" The brahman answered: "The people in this world are blind. They do not see anything; so I carry a torch in order to illuminate them." Considering the ways of the world, there was none who dared to speak up. The Buddha knew that the brahman should be saved because of his previous merits. Still, his behavior was haughty, seeking dominance and fame. He did not take impermanence into account. His self-conceit and arrogance were such that he would fall into the hell of [the lord of] Mount T'ai for countless eons and to escape it would be very difficult. So the Buddha transformed himself into a worthy and sat down in the marketplace. Then he asked the brahman why he was acting in this way. The brahman replied: "Because people are in darkness and cannot distinguish clearly between night and day, I illuminate them with the flame of my torch." The worthy again asked the brahman:

579a "Among the scriptural texts are the four *Vedas*. Do you know their essential teachings?" He replied: "I have no clear idea. What are their four essential teachings?" The worthy said: "One, harmonization of the four seasons through knowledge of astronomy and geography. Two, distinction of the five elements through knowledge of the constellations. Three, being able to pacify the country through knowledge of government. Four, unfailing firmness through knowledge of military affairs. You are a brahman. Don't you possess these teachings of the four *Vedas*?" The brahman was ashamed. He threw away his torch and crossed his hands. His thoughts were not up to it. The Buddha knew what was on his mind, and transformed himself back into his own self. His light shone brightly on both heaven and earth. With a divine voice he then spoke this stanza to the brahman:

> 5. If one has limited learning and considers oneself so
> great as to be arrogant toward others, then the one who
> holds the torch is the blind one. He illuminates others but
> does not illuminate himself.

After the Buddha had spoken the stanza, he said to the brahman: "No one is in more complete darkness than you, but you have entered a great country with a torch in your hand during the daytime. How much like a speck of dust is your knowledge!" When the brahman heard this, he blushed in shame. He immediately kowtowed and wished to be his disciple. The Buddha accepted him and let him become an ascetic. His thoughts were resolved, his foolishness ended, and he became an arhat.

Once there was an important elder in the land of Śrāvastī. His name was Sudatta and he had obtained the status of a stream-enterer. He had a friend, an elder called Hao-shih, who did not believe in the Buddha's path or in any therapeutic technique. He happened one day to fall seriously ill. Failing in energy, he had to keep to his bed. His relatives and friends all went to ask how he was. They insisted that he seek treatment, but he would not agree at all. He replied to everyone: "I have served the sun and moon and been loyal and pious toward the ruler and my father. Even if my life were to end here, I shall never change my mind." Sudatta said to him: "The teacher I serve is called the Buddha. His divine qualities spread far and wide. Those who see him gain good fortune. You might try and invite him to expound the scriptures and intone the incantations. Listen to what he says! What your words and behavior have led up to, how can they be better than some other path! Whether you follow it or not, that is up to you. Because your illness will last and will not get better soon, I insist that you invite the Buddha, and I hope you will receive his good fortune." As the day was auspicious, Hao-shih [said:] "You may invite the Buddha and his disciples for me." Sudatta immediately invited the Buddha and his Sangha. As he went to the elder's home, the Buddha emitted a bright light that penetrated everywhere. When the elder saw the light, he felt happy and relieved. The Buddha went to him and sat down. He asked the elder how his illness was, which spirits he had served before, and which therapy he had applied. The elder said to the Buddha: "I have served the sun and moon, my ruler, superiors, and ancestors. I respect the ordinances for abstention and I pray for all kinds of matters. I have had this illness for quite some time, but I have not received any blessings yet. Healing herbs, acupuncture, and cauterization are taboo for us. The merits of the precepts in the scriptures have

579b heretofore been unknown to me. Since my forefathers' time we have followed these practices until we die." The Buddha said to the elder: "When one is born into the world, there are three kinds of untimely death. To have a disease that does not heal is the first untimely death. To heal but not to be cautious is the second untimely death. To be haughty and self-satisfied and not to apprehend what is adverse or favorable is the third untimely death. Such illnesses cannot be done away with by the sun or the moon, by heaven or earth, or by serving forefathers, one's ruler, or one's father. It will be relieved in time through the path of knowledge. First, the temperature of the four elements requires healing herbs. Second, the evil demons of any heresy require the precepts of the scriptures. Third, serving the noble relieves misery, virtue affects the spirits, and merit helps beings. Remove the hindrance of the five aggregates through great knowledge! When one behaves thus, one is happy in the present world and there will never be anything untimely. Purified by morality and wisdom, one will always be in peace from generation to generation." Thereupon the World-honored One spoke the stanzas:

> 6. One serves the sun because of its light and one serves
> one's father out of gratitude. One serves one's ruler
> because of his power. One serves a man of the Path
> because of his learning.

> 7. One serves a doctor because of one's life. If one wants to
> win, one relies on vigor. The Doctrine resides in wisdom.
> Meritorious conduct is always clear.

> 8. One examines one's friends when making plans, and
> one leaves one's companion in case of urgency. One looks
> on one's wife when happy in the bedchamber. If one
> wants to know, knowledge lies in the discourses.

> 9. An able teacher shows the Path. He resolves doubts so
> that one may commend clear learning. He also cleanses
> the foundations of purity, ably maintaining the store-
> house of the Doctrine.

10. Learning brings benefit to wife and child, to elders
and younger brothers, and to friends in the present world.
It also brings about merit for the later world. Through the
accumulation of learning, one becomes noble and wise.

11. Because one can comprehend it, one may understand
what is meaningful. With understanding, the precepts
will not be broken. He who has received the Doctrine and
maintains it will accordingly quickly achieve tranquility.

12. He will be able to disperse sorrowful distress and do
away with ominous decay. If you wish to secure tranquility and prosperity, you must serve the learned.

When the elder had heard the Buddha's exposition of the Doctrine, the fetters of doubt in his mind quickly dispersed like clouds.
Like a skillful physician in practice, he devoted his mind to the
qualities of the Path. His four elements were at peace, and any
distress disappeared, as if he had drunk nectar. He was inwardly
and externally delighted, his body in peace and his mind settled.
He obtained the path of the stream-enterer. His kindred and countrymen all served him with reverence.

There were once vast mountains in the south of the land of
Rājaghṛa, two hundred miles away from the city. The roads to
every country in the south passed through these mountains. They
were treacherous and deep, and infested by five hundred bandits
who robbed the people traveling through the passes. Afterwards
the spoils were freely scattered about. The merchants were ruined and the king's way blocked. The king pursued the bandits to
punish them, but he could not capture them. The Buddha was in
the land then, and felt pity for the people, considering that those 579c
bandits did not know evil from good. [He thought:] "The Tathāgata
is in the world, but their eyes do not see him. The drum of the
Dharma is beaten every day, but their ears do not hear it. If I do
not go to save them, they will fall like rocks into an abyss." He
changed into a man wearing splendid clothes. He rode a horse and

had a sword on his waist and a bow and arrows in his hands. His saddle and bridle were decorated, adorned with gold and silver, and he let bright moon-pearls hang down from his horse. Making music on horseback, he went into the mountains. When bandits saw him, they thought the job was as good as done. They had been bandits for many years but had not yet had such an opportunity as this. Would this be any different from throwing eggs at a rock? The whole band of bandits got together and surrounded the traveler. They pulled their bows and drew their swords. While they were arguing about which one would strip him clean, the transformed person raised his bow and shot once, with the result that the five hundred bandits were all hit by arrows. He pointed at them with his sword and all of them were wounded. Their wounds were serious, the arrows struck deep, and they all fell down. All five hundred bandits lay twisting on the ground. They kowtowed and submitted. "What spirit are you, that you have such supernatural powers? We beg you for forgiveness so that we may keep our insignificant lives. Please, quickly pull out the arrows so that the wounds may heal! Our wounds now hurt unbearably." The transformed person answered: "These wounds do not hurt. The arrows are not deep. No wound is more serious in the world than sorrow. There is no injury worse than foolishness. So long as you cherish the sorrows of greed and injurious thoughts, your sword wounds and poisonous arrow wounds can never heal. The roots of these two things are much deeper. The valiant and the strong cannot pull them out. Only when one possesses the moral prescripts of the scriptures and becomes learned in the meaningfulness of wisdom, can this path of insight cure mental diseases. These prescripts remove sorrowful craving, foolishness, and haughtiness. They suppress violence, luxury, and covetousness. If you accumulate qualities and apply yourselves to wisdom, they may be done away with and you will forever gain tranquility." Thereupon the transformed person appeared as the Buddha. His [thirty-two] primary and [eighty] secondary auspicious marks stood out, and his shining face was very beautiful. He spoke the stanzas:

13. Among the wounds that afflict you none is worse than sorrow; and among the arrows shot none is worse than foolishness. The strong cannot pull them out. They are only removed by learning.

14. The blind gain their sight through it, and one in darkness obtains a candle. It leads people in the world, just as someone who sees leads those who do not see.

15. Therefore one who gives up delusion, who is free from pride and the joy of luxury, who applies himself and serves the learned, he is called the one who has accumulated virtues.

When the five hundred men saw the Buddha's shining appearance and had also heard these stanzas, they kowtowed and took refuge in him. They subdued their thoughts and repented. Meanwhile, the sword's wounds and poisonous arrows were removed by themselves. They were happy and their minds opened up to accept the five precepts. The whole realm was tranquil and suffused in happiness.

Chapter IV

Earnest Faith

580a There was once a big river southeast of the city of Śrāvastī. Its waters were deep and wide. More than five hundred families lived along its banks. They had not yet heard about the qualities of the Path or the way of salvation from the worldly. Their manners were violent, and they were busy cheating each other. They coveted gain, and were licentious, rash, and extremely willful. The World-honored One constantly thought he should go there to save those among them who should be saved. He knew that these families should be saved by their merits. Thereupon the World-honored One went to the riverbank and sat down under a tree. When the villagers saw the Buddha's bright appearance, they found it extraordinary, and there was none who was not impressed. They all went to pay their respects. Some saluted and some bowed, asking how he was. The Buddha told them to sit down, and he expounded the Doctrine of the scriptural texts. The crowd heard it, but they did not believe in it because they were used to fraud and were skeptical of any true words. The Buddha then magically caused someone to appear, coming from the south of the river. Walking on the water, just wet to his ankles, he came to the Buddha. He kowtowed and greeted the Buddha. When the crowd saw this, there was none who was not astonished. They asked the transformed person: "From the time of our ancestors we have lived on these shores, yet we have never heard of anyone walking on water. Who are you, sir? What kind of magic do you have that you are able to tread on water and not drown? Please explain it to us." The transformed person answered: "I am a foolish person from

35

south of the river. When I heard that the Buddha was here, I wanted to enjoy the virtues of the Path, but when I arrived at the southern shore, I could not cross in time. I asked someone on the shore whether the water was deep or shallow. He said: 'The water may reach up to your ankles. Why do you not wade across?' I trusted his words and just crossed over like that. There is nothing strange or miraculous about it." The Buddha then said in praise: "Excellent! Excellent! If you have faith, you may truly cross the abyss of birth and death. Why be astonished about walking across a river that is a few *li* wide?" Thereupon the World-honored One spoke the stanzas:

> 1. Faith can cross over any abyss. Restraint is the captain. Vigorous pursuit removes suffering, and wisdom lets you reach the other shore.

> 2. If one practices devout conduct, one is praised by the noble. One who enjoys the unconditioned is delivered from any bond.

> 3. With faith the Path can be obtained. The Doctrine engenders cessation. Through learning wisdom is obtained. In what is attained there is clearness.

> 4. When the alert mind practices faith and morality well, the strong man surpasses hate, and so he is freed from the abyss.

When the villagers heard the Buddha's exposition, their faith was realized. Their minds opened up and their faith was firm. They all received the five precepts and became people of pure faith. As their pure faith was developed, the teaching of the Doctrine was spread throughout the world.

Long ago, when the Buddha was in the world, there was an important elder called Hsiu-lo-t'o (Surādha?). His wealth was immeasurable and he was devoutly attuned to the qualities of the Path. He had vowed that he would always invite the Buddha and his

Sangha on the eighth day of the twelfth month, and that after his
death his son and grandson would always honor the vow. When
the elder was dying, he ordered his son not to abandon the practice. His son was called Pi-lo-t'o (Virādha?). Later he became poorer
and poorer and had nothing in the house. When the twelfth month
arrived, he had nothing to offer. He was sad and unhappy. The
Buddha sent Maudgalyāyana to go and ask Virādha: "The month
of your father's obligation is coming; what plans do you have?"
Virādha answered: "My late father gave me instructions, and I
do not dare oppose him. I hope that the World-honored One does
not think that I suddenly discarded them! On the eighth day at
noon he may radiate his brightness and have a closer look!"
Maudgalyāyana then returned and reported everything. Virādha
then took his wife to his father-in-law to borrow a hundred taels
of gold. On his returning home he provided for everything. The
Buddha went to his house with one thousand two hundred fifty
monks. When they had taken their seats, they passed the water
around and ate. Having cleansed themselves, they returned to their
pure abode. Virādha was glad and did not feel any contrition. On
that day, in the middle of the night, precious objects replenished
his storehouse, filling it as in the past. When Virādha and his wife
saw this the next morning, they were glad but also afraid. They
were afraid that officials might see the treasures and ask where
they had come from. Husband and wife discussed the matter [and
decided] that he should go and ask the Buddha. So he went to the
Buddha and explained the whole situation. The Buddha told
Virādha: "Put your mind at rest and feel free to use these treasures! Do not be suspicious! By your devout conduct you did not
offend against your father's instructions. Your morality, shame,
and moral dread have remained the same since his death. With
learning, giving, and the path of wisdom, you are endowed the
seven riches in their entirety. This has been brought about by
your merits and is in no way a calamity. When a wise person can
develop [these seven riches], no matter whether one is a man or a

woman or where one's place of birth is, a meritorious reward follows by itself." Thereupon the World-honored One spoke the stanzas:

> 5. Faith is wealth and morality is wealth. Shame and moral dread are riches too. Learning is wealth and giving is wealth. Wisdom is the seventh wealth.

> 6. Through faith one guards morality, [keeping it] constantly pure when contemplating. Walking in wisdom, one serves the teaching and does not forget it.

> 7. When one has these riches in life, no matter whether one is a man or a woman, one is never poor. The wise know this to be true.

When Virādha heard the Buddha's explanation, his earnest faith increased. He kowtowed at the Buddha's feet and returned home with joy. He made a complete analysis of the Buddha's teaching and instructed his wife and children. They then carried it out and all attained the Path.

Chapter V

Morality

Long ago there were mountains in the land of Benares about forty or fifty *li* away from the city. Five ascetics lived in the mountains, applying themselves to the Path. At dawn they left the mountains to beg for food. After they had eaten, they returned to the mountains, arriving at dusk. Going and returning was so very wearisome that they were not able to sit in meditation and develop right concentration. For years it was like that and they could not obtain the Path. The Buddha felt compassion for their fruitless efforts. He changed into a man of the Path and went to them. He asked these men aspiring for the Path if it was not too hard to develop the Path dwelling in seclusion. The ascetics responded: "We are already far away from the city. Our body with its four elements needs food and drink. We are exhausted from the trips for our daily provisions. For years and years we have suffered. We go and return in the daytime, but in the evening we are just too tired. We have no time to develop the Path any more. It will be just like that all our lives." The man of the Path said: "Well, he who considers the Path should take morality as its basis and mental restraint as its practice, but if you despise the body while valuing the truth, you will reject your corporal life. So sustain your body with food and guard your mind in right concentration! If you internally apply yourself to tranquility and insight, you will appease your mind and attain the Path. How can one avoid hardship without properly nourishing oneself! Please, men aspiring for the Path, do not go tomorrow! I shall give you nourishment, so that you may rest one day." So, the five ascetics were very happy, marveling at this wonder. With appeased thoughts and a settled mind, they did not worry about going to beg any more. At noon the next day the transformed man of the Path came to bring them food. After their meal they were content, their minds tranquil. Thereupon the transformed man expounded the stanzas:

1. When a monk is established morally, he restrains his faculties. Knowing temperance in eating, he applies himself with an alert mind.

2. Subduing his thoughts with moral conduct, he preserves proper concentration of mind. Internally practicing tranquility and insight, he is free from forgetfulness and has right knowledge.

3. When a wise one guards his moral nature, he internalizes right knowledge. When he practices the Path accordingly, he purifies himself and removes suffering.

When the transformed man of the Path had spoken these stanzas, he manifested the bright characteristics of the Buddha's body. Thereupon the five ascetics were spiritually moved. Grateful for his kindness, they kept the precepts and obtained arhatship.

Chapter VI

Mindfulness

When the Buddha was once in the world, King Pukkaśati and King Bimbisāra were friends. King Pukkaśati did not yet know the Buddha's Path. He made seven precious bouquets and sent them to King Bimbisāra. Upon receiving them, King Bimbisāra in turn presented them to the Buddha. He said to the Buddha: "King Pukkaśati is a good friend of mine and he has sent me these flowers. I now present them to you, O Buddha. Please, let the mind of that king open up and make him understand! Let him see you, O Buddha, hear your Doctrine, and respect the noble Sangha! With what shall I respond to what he has sent me?" The Buddha informed King Bimbisāra: "Copy the scriptural text on the twelve causes and present it to him. Upon receiving the scriptural text, his mind is sure to turn to zealous devotion." He then copied the scriptural text and added a letter, saying: "You sent me precious flowers. I now present you this bouquet of the Doctrine. Carefully reflect on its meaning! Its [doctrine of] retribution is very good. When you are well versed in its recitation, you will share in the flavor of the Path." When King Pukkaśati received the scriptural text, he read and reflected on it again and again, and quickly became zealously devoted. He sighed deeply and said: "My conversion to the Path is truly wonderful. Its essence means pacification of the spirit and the glory of the state. The five sensual desires are the source of sorrow. For eons I have erred. Only now do I awaken! If one exam- 581a ines current customs, there is nothing to enjoy." So he summoned his ministers, entrusted the state to the crown prince, shaved his head, and became an ascetic. Donning the robe of the Dharma and

41

with alms bowl in hand, he went to a potter's home outside the city of Rājagṛha to spend the night. The following day he went to the city to beg, and after he had eaten he went to the Buddha to receive the precepts. The Buddha knew with supernatural knowledge that Pukkaśati's life would end the following day at mealtime and that he therefore should not come from so far away to meet with him. Furthermore, it would be a great pity if he did not hear the scriptures. Thereupon the World-honored One transformed himself into an ascetic. He went to the potter and asked permission to spend the night. The potter said: "There is an ascetic who came earlier. You may stay with him in the pottery there." He took some straw, entered the pottery, and sat down to one side. He asked Pukkaśati where he came from, who his teacher was, why he had become an ascetic, and if he had met the Buddha yet. Pukkaśati said: "I have not met the Buddha yet. When I learned about the twelve causes, I became an ascetic. Tomorrow I shall enter the city and after my meal of alms food I shall go to meet the Buddha!" The transformed ascetic said: "Man's life is hazardous, with changes occurring from morning till night. In its impermanence, the retribution of past deeds emerges all of a sudden, and not at any fixed time. Just observe your body as a coming together of the four great elements. It is the result of their combination as well as their dissipation, each returning to its origin. Develop an awakened mind characterized by emptiness, purity, and thoughtlessness. Be especially mindful of the three respectful doctrines [Buddha, Dharma, and Sangha] and of giving and the quality of morality. To know impermanence is no different from meeting the Buddha. Your thinking of tomorrow is a profitless thought." The transformed ascetic then spoke the stanzas:

1. If someone with considerable possessions has come to take refuge in the Buddha, he must day and night constantly be mindful of the Buddha, his Dharma, and his Sangha.

2. Those who know and have awakened their minds are the disciples of the Buddha. Day and night they are constantly mindful of the Buddha, Dharma, and Sangha.

3. Be mindful of your body and its impermanent nature! Be mindful of morality and the virtue of giving! Day and night be mindful of emptiness, aimlessness, and signlessness.

The transformed ascetic in the pottery then expounded the essence of impermanence to Pukkaśati. When King Pukkaśati developed his mental concentration, he gained the path of a non-returner (*anāgāmin*). When the Buddha knew that the king understood, he manifested the splendor and auspicious luminous marks of his Buddha body. King Pukkaśati was surprised and in rapture. He kowtowed and did obeisance. The Buddha again informed him: "The retribution of evil is impermanent. Do not be afraid when it is over!" When King Pukkaśati said: "I have respectfully received your teaching, O Reverend," he suddenly went away. The following day, when it was time to eat, King Pukkaśati entered the city to beg for alms food. At the gate of the city, he encountered a cow that had just borne her young. Protecting her calf, she butted against King Pukkaśati to kill him. His belly was split open and his life ended. He was immediately reborn in the non-returner heaven. The Buddha sent his disciples to cremate 581b him and erect a stupa. The Buddha said to his disciples: "It is impossible not to heed the basis of the retribution of evil."

Chapter VII

Kindness

Once the Buddha was in Rājagṛha and mountains existed five hundred *li* away. In the mountains there was a family of one hundred twenty-two members whose occupation was hunting in the marshes of the mountains. They wore furs and ate meat, and had never cultivated the land. They served the spirits and did not know about the Buddha, Dharma, and Sangha. With noble insight the Buddha knew that they could be saved. He went to the family and sat down under a tree. The men had gone off to hunt and only the women were there. When they saw the Buddha's bright appearance illuminating heaven and earth, and the trees and rocks in the mountains changing to gold, the young and old were ecstatic. Knowing that the Buddha was a supernatural person, they all went to pay their respects, brought offerings, and sat down. The Buddha explained to the mothers the wrong of killing living beings, the merit of practicing kindness, and that any affection between two persons is momentary and any union will soon end in parting. Upon hearing the scriptural text, the mothers rejoiced and said to the Buddha: "We mountain people are eager to take life in order to have meat to eat. We want to present some to you as a small offering. We hope you will accept it." The Buddha informed the mothers: "It is the rule of any Buddha not to eat meat. As I have already had my meal, you need not provide anything else." He then instructed them: "When man is born in the world, he has food without limit. Why does he not make use of beneficial food but instead does away with living things to stay alive himself? When he dies he falls into a woeful destination, and being hurt he gains no benefit. When man eats the five cereals, he feels pity for living beings and the wriggling species. There is no creature that does not want to live. When one kills others to keep oneself alive, calamitous evil does not end. When one is compassionate and does not kill, one is without calamity from generation to generation." Thereupon the World-honored One spoke the following stanzas:

> 1. He who is compassionate and does not kill, and who can constantly control himself, dwells in immortality. He is in a place where there is no calamity.

> 2. He who does not kill and is compassionate, who is cautious in his speech and guards his thoughts, dwells in immortality. He is in a place where there is no calamity.

> 3. He who graciously does not interfere, who does not harm living beings and who does not annoy anyone, deserves the brahma heaven.

> 4. He who is always compassionate and pure, in accordance with the teachings of the Buddha, experiences satisfaction and quietude. He transcends birth and death.

When the Buddha had spoken the stanzas, the men returned from their hunting. Their women were listening to the scriptures and did not go to welcome them as was the custom. The husbands were suspicious and they wondered why things were not as usual. They abandoned the meat and came back [to the village] thinking that something strange was going on. They came back and saw that all the women were sitting in front of the Buddha listening to the scriptures with folded hands. They became angry and drew their bows, intent on destroying the Buddha. But the women remonstrated, saying: "He is a supernatural person. Do not give rise to any evil thoughts!" Therefore each repented his sins and did obeisance to the Buddha. The Buddha again explained to them the merit of not killing and the evil of doing harm. The husbands understood, knelt deeply, and said to the Buddha: "We grew up deep in the mountains, maintaining ourselves by hunting. Our evil

581c

misdeeds have accumulated. Which rule should we follow in order to escape grave misfortune?" Thereupon the World-honored One spoke the stanzas:

> 5. Acting kindly and compassionately, and saving beings with universal love, one gains the eleven praises, and good fortune always follows.

> 6. When sleeping or awake he is at peace with himself. He does not have bad dreams. The gods protect him, and he is loved by others. He is not rebuked nor met with hostilities.

> 7. He does not perish by water or by fire. He obtains gain wherever he is, and when dead he ascends to the brahma heaven. These are the eleven [praises].

When the Buddha had spoken the stanzas, the one hundred twenty-two men and women, young and old, were glad and devoutly accepted them. They all subscribed to the five precepts. The Buddha told King Bimbisāra to give them land and to present them with cereals. The conversion to benevolence was widespread, and throughout the land there was peace.

Once there was a great king called Ho-mo. Living in a border region, he had not yet seen the noble and wonderful conversion possible through the Buddha, Dharma, and Sangha. He served brahmans and heretics, and conducted sorcery. The whole country was heretical in that living beings were killed as sacrifices. This was considered to be the rule. Then the king's mother fell ill. Failing in energy, she had to keep to her bed. He sent for doctors, but he did not receive any medical drafts. He sent for wise women, seeking for them everywhere. After many years, she had still to recover. He again summoned the brahmans in the land and some two hundred people came. He invited them in, had them sit down, offered them food and drink, and informed them: "My mother has been ill for a long time. I do not know what brought this about. You have great knowledge and clear understanding of the principles of physiognomy and of heaven and earth and its constellations.

Why is it that you are unable to tell me what to do?" The brahmans said: "The constellations stand in the wrong position and yin and yang are not in harmony. That is why this has occurred." The king said: "What is the right thing to do so that she may recover?" The brahmans said: "In a peaceful and pure place outside of the city you should sacrifice to the four mountains, and to the sun and moon and the constellations. You should obtain a hundred animals of all kinds, including a boy, kill them, and offer them to heaven. O king, you should personally lead your mother there, and kneel and do obeisance and beg for her life. Only then will she recover." So the king provided them as instructed. As the boy and a hundred head of elephants, horses, cows, and sheep were driven, they cried out sadly along the way, moving heaven and earth. Leaving through the eastern gate, the king was going to the sacrificial altar to kill and offer them to heaven. As the World-honored One's great compassion saves all beings, he pitied this king's utter foolishness. "How can he give rise to evil by killing many beings in order to save one person!" Thereupon the World-honored One led his great assembly to this land. At the eastern gate of the city he met the king and the brahmans on their way out. The animals they were driving came out, crying sadly. The king saw the Buddha in the distance, like the sun that has just risen or the full moon. His radiance brightly lit up heaven and
582a earth. When the people saw him, they were all filled with love and reverence. They all wanted to rid themselves of the animals they were driving as well as the sacrificial implements. The king then advanced and descended from his carriage. He removed his parasol and did obeisance to the Buddha. He crossed his fingers, knelt, and made inquiries to the World-honored One. The Buddha told him to rise and asked him where he was going. He folded his hands and answered: "The queen mother has been ill for a long time. I have consulted the finest physicians and the spirits everywhere. Now, I only want to go and allay the constellations, the four mountains, and the five sacred peaks. I shall beg for my mother's life, hoping that she may recover." The Buddha informed the great

king: "Listen well to these words! If you want to obtain cereals to eat, you must plow and sow. If you want to obtain great wealth, you must practice giving. If you want to obtain a long life, you must show great compassion. If you want to obtain wisdom, you must apply yourself to learning. If you practice these four things, you will gain their fruits as they are sown. A wealthy and honorable family does not covet the food of the humble. The gods take the seven precious things for their abode. Their clothing and food come naturally. Why should they forsake an ambrosial meal to take coarse food! Sacrificing to licentiousness is like considering what is wrong to be right. If one kills life to seek life, one is far from the path of life. If one kills the life of many in order to save one person, how could one succeed that way?" Thereupon the World-honored One spoke the stanza:

> 8. If one lives a hundred years, diligently serving the spirits in the world, the sacrifice of elephants and horses would not be the same as one act of compassion.

When the Buddha had spoken the stanza, he cast a bright glow that illuminated heaven and earth. All in the three woeful destinations and in the eight inopportune births were happy, each one in his place. King Ho-mo heard the exposition of the wonderful Doctrine, and he saw the bright glow. He was overjoyed and obtained the Path. When his sick mother heard the Doctrine, her five feelings lit up and her ailment disappeared. When the two hundred brahmans had seen the Buddha's bright appearance, and once again heard his words, they felt shame and regret, and they desired to become his disciples. The Buddha accepted them all, and they became ascetics, each one obtaining his wish. The king and his ministers invited the Buddha. When they had worshiped him for a month, he left. The king's rule was just, according to the Doctrine, and therein the land flourished.

Chapter VIII

Words

Once King Pukkaśati entered the city of Rājagṛha to beg for alms. At the gate of the city he was butted to death by a cow that had recently brought forth young. The owner of the cow was alarmed, and he sold the cow and turned it over to someone else. When that man was pulling the cow to water it, the cow again butted its master to death from behind. That owner had a son who became extremely angry. He took the cow to be killed and sold the meat in the market. There was a farmer who bought the head of the cow. He carried it with a rope over his shoulder and took it home. Further than a *li* from his home he sat down under a tree to rest and hung the head of the cow from a branch. After a while the rope broke and the cow's head fell right on top of him. The cow's horns pierced him and his life immediately ended. In one day the cow had killed a total of three people.

582b

When King Bimbisāra heard this, he wondered why. So he went with his ministers to where the Buddha was. After he had done obeisance upon arrival, he sat apart on the king's throne. He folded his hands and said to the Buddha: "Very odd it is, O World-honored One, that one cow kills three people. Because the event is sure to be [regarded as] something strange, I wish to hear the meaning of this." The Buddha informed King Bimbisāra: "The retribution of a misdemeanor has an origin. It does not happen just now." The king said: "I would like to hear the reason." The Buddha said: "Long ago there were three merchants who went to another country to make a living. They stayed in the house of an aged widow. They had to pay rent, but when they saw that the

51

old woman was a widow, they cheated her and they did not want to pay. They watched when the old woman was not in and they left without a word, not paying the rent. When the old woman returned and did not see the merchants, she asked her neighbors, who said they had all gone. The old woman was furious. So she went looking for them, and after a wearisome pursuit she caught up with them and demanded the rent for the house. The three merchants scolded her instead, saying: 'We already paid you. Why do you ask again?' They all as one contradicted her and they did not want to pay the rent. The old woman was alone and weak and could not do anything. Cursing them angrily she said to the three merchants: 'I may be in distress now, but why should I bear your cheating rebuttal! As for me, I vow that if I shall meet you in the place where I shall later be reborn, I shall certainly kill you so that you may obtain the right path! I shall never forget you! I shall rest when I have killed you. Until then, I will not stop!'" The Buddha said to King Bimbisāra: "The old woman at that time is now this cow. The three merchants are the three people, Pukkaśati and the others, who were butted to death by the cow." Thereupon the World-honored One spoke the stanzas:

1. When one uses evil words and scolds, is arrogant and despises others, when one engenders such behavior, hatred grows and grows.

2. When one speaks humbly and affably, respects others, rejects the bonds, and bears the harshness, hatred is naturally appeased.

3. When a man is born, there is an ax in his mouth. The reason why he destroys himself is because of his evil words.

When the Buddha had explained this, all those in King Bimbisāra's official retinue were full of respect and vowed to dedicate themselves to good conduct. They did obeisance and departed.

Chapter IX

Fundamentals in Pairs

Once the king of the land of Śrāvastī, called Prasenajit, came to where the Buddha was. He descended from his carriage, withdrew his parasol, removed his sword, took off his footwear, folded his hands, and came forward. He prostrated himself, kowtowed at his feet, knelt deeply, and said to the Buddha: "I wish to arrange for a trifling meal tomorrow at the four thoroughfares. I want to let people know that you, the Buddha, are most honored. I wish to make beings forsake demons and sorcery and have them all follow the five precepts in order to avert calamities to the state!" The 582c Buddha said: "Excellent! Well, as the state sovereign you should have intelligent leadership and lead your people along the Path seeking future blessedness!" The king said: "With utmost sincerity, I ask leave to make strict preparations." He prepared delicacies with his own hands and went by himself to receive the Buddha and his monks. When they had all arrived at the four thoroughfares, the Buddha came there and took his seat. [The king] passed around water so that they could cleanse themselves, and he poured it with his own hands. When the Buddha had finished his meal, he expounded the Doctrine to the king at the four crossroads. Among the countless onlookers at that time were two merchants. One thought: "The Buddha is like an emperor. His disciples are like loyal ministers. The Buddha explains his bright Doctrine and his disciples proclaim it. This king is bright! Knowing that the Buddha is honorable, he submits and serves him." The other one thought: "This king is foolish! He is the king of the land. What more could he want? The Buddha is like an ox, and his disciples are like a cart. The ox pulls the cart in all four directions. The Buddha is just like that. What reason would you have to submit to and serve him?" Both men went away, and after a journey of thirty *li* they stopped and lodged for the night. Buying some wine, they drank together and discussed their affairs. The four kings protected the one who had had wholesome thoughts, but the evil spirits on Mount T'ai let the wine enter the belly of the one who had had unwholesome thoughts, burning him like fire. He left the inn and lay down on the road. He sprawled out in the wheel tracks, but in the morning five hundred merchant carts rode over him there and he died. When his companion looked for him the next day, he found him dead. He said: "When I return to my country, I shall be suspected of having killed him to take away his belongings. There is no sense in taking this lightly." So he abandoned the riches and went to another country.

The king of this land had died without a crown prince. In the Book of Prophecies it says: "In the central region there is a humble person who will rule this land. The former king has a divine horse, which is sure to bend its knees when a new king is appointed." They immediately prepared a stately carriage, the divine horse, and the ribbon for the official seal, and they went looking for the [new] sovereign of the land. They saw thousands, but the merchant still stood out. The national astronomer said: "He has a yellow cloud cover; this is the aura of a ruler." The divine horse bent its knees and licked the feet of the merchant. The officials prepared fragrant hot water, bathed him, and saluted him as their king. Thereupon he occupied the throne and tended to the affairs of the state. Deep inside himself he thought: "I do not have the slightest aptitude. Why did I obtain this [position]? It must be the Buddha's kindness that has brought this about." He then went to the land of Śrāvastī with his officials. He kowtowed from a distance and said: "I do not have any merit to receive your kindness, O World-honored One, or to rule over this land. I wish to be kind to the multitude of worthies (arhats) tomorrow and to look after them."

Once, in the third month, the Buddha informed Ānanda and ordered his monks: "Tomorrow you are invited by that king. You must all transform yourselves so that the king and his people will rejoice!" They each used the foundations of their supernatural power to go to that country. They all took their seats in the proper order, dignified and according to the rules. After they had eaten, they washed their hands and expounded the Doctrine to the king. The king said: "I am actually an insignificant person. I never had any virtue to speak of. Why did I come to this [position]?" The Buddha informed the king: "Once that great king gave food to me, to the Buddha, at the four thoroughfares. You, O King, thought: 'The Buddha is like a king. His disciples are like his ministers.' You, O King, sowed this seed. Now you obtain its fruition. The other person said that the Buddha was like an ox and that his disciples were like a cart. He sowed the calamity of being run over by a cart. Now he is in the hell of Mount T'ai, run over by a blazing chariot and obtaining his deserts. It is not your vigor, O King, that could bring this about. If one does something wholesome, merit follows. If one does something evil, misfortune follows. This is one's own doing, and it cannot be given by gods, dragons, or spirits." Thereupon the World-honored One spoke the stanzas: 583a

> 1. The mind is the origin of everything. The eminence of the mind is caused by the mind. If one thinks of evil, either of word or deeds, the suffering of sin naturally follows, as a wagon's wheels leave their tracks.

> 2. The mind is the origin of everything. The eminence of the mind is caused by the mind. If one thinks of good, either of words or of deeds, the happiness of merits naturally follows, as the shadow follows the form.

When the Buddha had spoken the scriptural stanzas, those who had heard them, the king and his subjects, were innumerable. They were all very glad and obtained the eye of the Doctrine.

Long ago the elder Sudatta bought some land from the crown prince. Together they built a pure abode and presented it to the World-honored One. Each invited the Buddha and his Sangha and made offerings for one month. The Buddha gave an extensive exposition of the luminous Doctrine to both men, and they both attained the Path. The crown prince, Jeta, was glad, and he returned to his eastern palace. Praising the Buddha's qualities, he made music and rejoiced. Jeta's younger brother, Virūḍhaka, was always at the king's side. The king then dressed up in plain clothes and, with his courtiers and ladies in waiting, went to where the Buddha was. After he had kowtowed and done obeisance, he intently listened to the scriptures. Virūḍhaka stayed behind and was in charge of the throne. His deceitful ministers, Aśraddha and others, then hatched a treacherous plot, and they said: "Try to wear the great king's ribbon with his official seal, and sit on the throne! Would you not be just like the king?" Thereupon Virūḍhaka agreed with their words. He donned the robe and mounted the throne. The deceitful ministers all congratulated him: "You are just like the great king! May you meet with the people's good wishes for a thousand years! Why, let the one of the eastern palace seek [the throne]! How could he mount this throne and then step down!" Virūḍhaka immediately took the leadership over his followers, put on his armor, drew his sword, and went to the pure abode of the Jetavana. He deposed the great king, blocking his return to the palace. He battled the king's subjects in the Jetavana and killed more than five hundred of the king's courtiers. The king fled with his ladies. At the earliest dawn they reached the country of the Śākyas. They became hungry along the way and the king ate radishes. His belly swelled and he died. Thereupon, Virūḍhaka became tyrannical. He drew his sword and entered the eastern palace to behead his elder brother, Jeta. Jeta knew his own impermanent nature. He was not afraid, and his countenance did not change color. He expressed gratification with a smile and he willingly submitted to the sword.

583b Before his life ceased, he heard natural music in the sky, welcoming his spirit. The Buddha then spoke the stanzas in the Jetavana:

> 3. He brings about joy and he will rejoice hereafter. The good-doer rejoices in both cases. He will rejoice, indeed be glad. Experiencing his merits, his mind is content.

4. Now he is glad and will hereafter be glad. The good-doer is glad in both cases. He brings about his own good fortune. Receiving his merits, he is delighted.

King Virūḍhaka then raised an army to attack the land of the Śākyas, and he killed the men of the Path of the Śākya family. In his cruelty and immorality he committed all five fatal transgressions. The Buddha predicted to Virūḍhaka that, as he was not filial and loyal and his sins were very grave, he would seven days later be burned by the fire of hell. The prediction of the chief prophesier further agreed with that of the Buddha. The king panicked. He boarded a ship and went to sea. [He thought:] "I am on water now. How could fire consume me!" At noon on the seventh day there was a spontaneous fire coming out of the water. It burned the ship and sank it. The king was burned too. Consumed by the vicious heat, he suddenly perished. Thereupon the World-honored One spoke the stanzas:

5. He brings about sorrow and he will grieve hereafter. The evildoer grieves in both cases. He will grieve, indeed be full of anxiety. Experiencing his sins, his mind is disturbed.

6. Now he repents and he will repent hereafter. The evildoer repents in both cases. He brings about his own misfortune. Experiencing his sins, he is tormented.

After the Buddha had expounded this, he informed the monks: "Crown prince Jeta did not covet a glorious position. He cherished the Path till death. He was reborn high in heaven and his happiness came of itself. King Virūḍhaka was foolish and he readily gave in to his desires. After his death he fell into hell and the suffering he experienced was immeasurable. The powerful and the poor throughout the world are subject to impermanence. There is none who stays long. And so, even the superior being died. His whole conduct was a spiritual treasure." When the Buddha had said this, there was none who did not accept it in faith.

Beyond Mount Gṛdhrakūṭa there once were more than seventy brahmans and their families who deserved to be saved because of their previous merits. The Buddha went to their village and appeared showing his supernatural power of the Path. When they all saw the majesty of the Buddha's bright appearance, they all respectfully bowed down. The Buddha sat down under a tree and asked the brahmans: "For how many generations have you lived in these mountains? What do you do to provide for your living?" They replied: "We have been living here for more than thirty generations. We farm and raise cattle." He further asked: "What practices do you observe with the aim of leaving [the cycle of] birth and death?" They replied: "We serve the sun and moon, water and fire. We observe timely sacrifices. If someone has died, young and old gather and pray for his rebirth in the brahma heaven, so that he may leave [the cycle of] birth and death." The Buddha said to the brahmans: "Farming and raising cattle, sacrificing to the sun and moon and to water and fire, and praying for rebirth in heaven are not the right ways to long life or to escape from the birth and death cycle. The highest merit [so achievable] does not go beyond the twenty-eight heavens. Without the wisdom of the Path, one falls back into the three woeful destinations. Only if one goes forth, develops his determination for purity, and practices what is meaningful for tranquility may one attain nirvana." Thereupon the World-honored One spoke the stanzas:

583c

> 7. Those who consider the real as unreal, and the unreal as real, have wrong thoughts and will not obtain real gain.

> 8. Those who know the real as real and who, upon seeing the unreal, know it to be unreal, will have right thoughts and will certainly obtain real gain.

> 9. Every generation knows death. In the three worlds there is no happiness. Although the gods are happy, they too will die when their merits have been exhausted.

> 10. When considering worldly matters, there is nothing produced that will not come to an end. Wanting to leave [the cycle of] birth and death, one must practice the true Path.

When the seventy brahmans had heard the Buddha's explanation, they understood and were glad, and they wished to become ascetics. The Buddha said: "Welcome, monks!" Their hair fell off of itself and they all became ascetics. The Buddha and the ascetics set out for the pure abode. When they were halfway there, they longed for their wives and children, and each wanted to withdraw. It happened to rain then, and they became even more depressed. The Buddha knew what was on their minds. He magically created several tens of huts along the way. They entered them to get out of the rain, but the huts were leaking. Because the huts were leaking, the Buddha spoke the stanzas:

> 11. If a house is ill thatched, it will leak when it rains. If the mind does not reflect on one's actions, it will be penetrated by lust.

> 12. If a house is well thatched, the rain will not leak through. If one reflects on one's actions with an attentive mind, lust is buried and does not arise.

Even though, upon hearing the exposition of these stanzas, the seventy ascetics did their best to pull themselves together, they still felt darkness in their hearts. The rain stopped and they went on their way. On the ground there was some old paper. The Buddha told a monk to pick it up. Being told so he picked it up. The Buddha asked the monks: "What kind of paper is this?" The monks said to the Buddha: "This is paper to wrap incense. It may be thrown away now, but it still retains its fragrance." The Buddha continued on his way. On the ground there was a broken string. The Buddha told a monk to pick it up. Being told so he picked it up. The Buddha further asked: "What kind of string is this?" The monks said: "That string is foul smelling. This is a string to tie up fish." The Buddha said to the monks: "These things are fundamentally pure, but they all depend on a cause to bring about what is wrong or meritorious. If you befriend a wise person, the meaning of the Path will be prominent. If you befriend an ignorant person, evil and misfortune will gather. It is like that paper or that string. When close to fragrance, it is fragrant. When used to tie up fish, it stinks. They are gradually tainted and become accustomed to it without being aware of it." Thereupon the World-honored One spoke the stanzas:

> 13. A vile person affects others, as if they were near a putrid thing. Gradually being deluded, they practice what is wrong, and, being unaware of it, they accomplish what is bad.

> 14. An excellent person affects others, as if they were near incense. Advancing in knowledge, they practice what is good, and bring about a clear scent.

584a When the seventy ascetics had heard these stanzas, they knew that the desire for home was a foul marsh, and that wife and children were fetters and handcuffs. With earnest faith they went to the pure abode. Reflecting on their actions with an attentive mind, they obtained the path of the arhat.

Chapter X

Negligence

Long ago, when the Buddha was in the world, there were five hundred merchants who had traveled the seas. They returned to their country carrying the seven precious things in large quantities. While passing deep through the mountains, they were misled by evil spirits and they could not find their way out. Their provisions were all used up; and placed in a distressing situation, they all subsequently died from hunger. The precious goods they were packing were scattered in the mountains. There was an ascetic then in the mountains, who was applying himself to the Path. Upon seeing this situation he thought to himself: "I have been diligent in my application to the Path for seven years, but I cannot attain it. Furthermore I am poor, without any means to sustain myself. These valuable goods do not have any owner. I shall take them back and establish a home." Thereupon he descended from the mountains and took precious things with him. After he had stored them away somewhere, he left the mountains. He asked his brothers to help him carry them back home. Just when he was halfway, the Buddha remembered that this monk would surely obtain deliverance. The Buddha then changed into a nun, with shaved head and the robe of the Doctrine, but with powdered face and painted eyebrows, and strung with necklaces of gold and silver. She entered the mountains through a valley and met the ascetic on her way. She made a deep bow and asked how he was doing. The man of the Path scolded the nun, saying: "Is this the way to attain the Path? One shaves the head and dons the robe of the Doctrine. But why still powder your face, paint your eyebrows, and wear necklaces on your person?" The nun answered: "Is this the way of an ascetic? He leaves his relatives, applies himself to the Path, dwells in the mountains, and appeases his mind. Why then take what is not yours? In your greed you are forgetful of the Path and quick to leave your noble intentions behind. You do not reckon with impermanence. Your birth in the world is like a journey, but the retribution for your evil is long-lasting." Thereupon the nun expounded to him the stanzas:

1. O monk, heed the precepts carefully! Negligence brings on great grief. In compensating strife, something small brings about something big. Through the accumulation of evil, one will burn in fire.

2. The merits of keeping the precepts lead to joy. Breaking the precepts, however, results in fearful thoughts. When one can do away with the impurities of the three worlds, one is close to nirvana.

Then, after the nun had spoken these stanzas, [the Buddha] showed [the monk] the brightness of the primary and secondary marks of his Buddha body. When the ascetic saw this, his hair stood on end with fear. He kowtowed at the Buddha's feet, repented his mistake, and pleaded: "A fool makes mistakes, acting contrary to the right teaching. When he goes on without redeeming himself, what will happen to him?" Thereupon the World-honored One spoke the stanzas:

584b

3. When one has earlier given way to negligence, but has later restrained himself well, he illuminates the world. Mindfulness to concentration is the proper attitude!

4. When one erringly has committed evil, but then overturns it by means of what is wholesome, he illuminates the world. Mindfulness to what is wholesome is the proper attitude!

5. He who, though young, goes forth from home and fully cultivates the Buddha's teaching illuminates the world as the moon does after the clouds have parted.

6. When one has earlier done evil, but has later ceased to
offend, he illuminates the world as the moon does after
the clouds have parted.

When the monk had heard these stanzas, his fetters were removed
and his covetousness ceased. He kowtowed at the Buddha's feet
and he went to sit under a tree. As his counting of breaths continued, his tranquility and insight became pure. He attained the re-
alization of the fruition of the Path and became an arhat.

Chapter XI

The Mind

Once, when the Buddha was in the world, there was a man of the Path. He sat under a tree on the bank of a river, and applied himself to the Path, but in twelve years his covetousness had not been conquered. Letting go his thoughts and with a distracted mind, he only held dear the six desires: beauty for his eyes, sounds for his ears, fragrances for his nose, flavors for his mouth, tactility for his body, and dharmas (elements) for his mind. His body was serene, but his mind wandered without any repose whatsoever. He had not been able to obtain the Path in twelve years; but the Buddha knew that he might be saved. He transformed himself into an ascetic and went to where the man was. They both lodged under a tree. On one occasion, by the light of the moon, a tortoise came out from the river to the tree. There also was a hungry otter looking for food. He saw the tortoise and wanted to eat it, but the tortoise drew in its head, tail, and four legs and hid them in its shell. It couldn't be eaten. When the otter was some distance away, the tortoise stuck out its head and feet and walked away. Nothing could be done about it, and so it got away. Thereupon the man of the Path said to the transformed ascetic: "This tortoise has an armor to protect its life. The otter could not gain advantage." The transformed ascetic replied: "I think that people in the world are inferior to this tortoise. Ignorant of their impermanence, they give rein to their six senses. When the external Māra gains advantage, the body is destroyed, and the spirit leaves. Birth and death cycles are endless, and revolve in the five destinations. Suffering is too immeasurable, all caused by the mind. One should exert oneself for external appeasement, seeking happiness." Thereupon the transformed ascetic spoke the stanzas:

> 1. The body does not last long. It will return to earth anyway. The body is destroyed and the spirit leaves. What would one desire by staying with it?

> 2. When thoughts seek to go somewhere, the coming and going is endless. If one has much viciousness in mind, one only provokes evil for himself.

> 3. A thought is created by oneself. It does not come from parents. You may direct it toward what is right! Do what is meritorious and do not turn back!

> 4. Hide your six [feelings], just like the tortoise! Guard your mind as a fortress! When wisdom is victorious in the battle with Māra, there will be no ailment.

584c

When the monk had heard the exposition of these stanzas, his covetousness ceased and his desire ended, and he attained the Path of an arhat. He knew that the transformed ascetic was the Buddha, the World-honored One. He reverentially adjusted his clothes and kowtowed at the Buddha's feet. All gods, dragons, and spirits were delighted.

Chapter XII

The Fragrance of Flowers

Once the Buddha was in the land of Śrāvastī. In the sea southeast of the country there was a terrace. On the terrace there were flowers and fragrant trees. The trees were pleasant. There were five hundred female brahmans who, although serving a heterodox path, were very diligent and zealous of the mind. They did not, however, know about the Buddha's existence. The women then said to each other: "When we received our forms we were born as women. From our youth until our old age, we are in the custody of three things, and we cannot be free. Furthermore, our life is brief. Our forms change as a mirage and will expire again. It would be better if we all went to the terrace with fragrant flowers to gather the fragrant flowers. If we are strenuous when fasting and let Brahmadeva descend, he will comply with our wishes. We wish to be reborn in the brahma heaven and to have a long life without death. We also [wish to be] free, without any bondage, freed from any retribution, and without any more sorrow." So they took their offerings and went to the terrace. They gathered fragrant flowers and served Brahmadeva. They held their fast wholeheartedly, wishing to let the venerable spirit descend.

Thereupon the World-honored One saw these women. Even though they held a lay fast, their minds were resolved and they deserved to be saved. So he flew up in the air with a great multitude of disciples, bodhisattvas, gods, *nāga*s, and spirits, went to the terrace, and sat down under a tree. The women were glad and they thought he was Brahmadeva. They comforted each other that they had obtained their wish. Then one celestial person said to the women: "This is not Brahmadeva. This is the most honored one in the three worlds, called the Buddha. The people he has saved are innumerable." Thereupon the women advanced to where the Buddha was. They did obeisance, came forward, and said to the Buddha: "We have a great deal of impurity and we are women now. We wish to be free from bondage and be reborn in the brahma heaven." The Buddha said: "O women, as you are eager to obtain fine gain, you have made this wish. In the world there are two things for which the retribution is clear. He who does what is wholesome experiences what is meritorious. He who does what is evil experiences calamity. The suffering of the world or the happiness of heaven, the vexation of the conditioned or the tranquility of the unconditioned, who can choose and take what is true? Excellent, O women, that you have a clear purpose!" Thereupon the World-honored One spoke the stanzas:

> 1. Who can choose the earth, reject custody, and choose heaven? Who can expound the verses of the Doctrine like picking wonderful flowers?

> 2. The learner chooses the earth, rejects custody, and chooses heaven. He expounds well the verses of the Doctrine and ably gathers the flowers of merit.

585a
> 3. Knowing that the world is like [breakable] earthenware, an illusion, and a brief existence, one brings a stop to the opening of Māra's flowers and will not experience the cycle of life and death.

> 4. Seeing the body like [evanescent] foam, an illusion, and spontaneous, one brings a stop to the opening of Māra's flowers and will not experience the cycle of life and death.

When the women had heard these stanzas of the Buddha, they wished to apply themselves to the true Path and to become nuns. Their hair fell off of itself and they were provided with the robe of the Doctrine. After reflection and quiet concentration they attained the path of the arhat. Ānanda said to the Buddha: "Well, what merit did these women actually have, that they had the World-honored One save them? And further, as soon as they had heard the exposition of the Doctrine, they went forth and attained the Path." The Buddha informed Ānanda: "Once, at the time of the Buddha Kāśyapa, there was an important elder whose riches were countless. His wives and ladies numbered five hundred. He was jealous by nature and his gate was not opened arbitrarily. The wives and ladies wanted to go and meet the Buddha, but they never obtained his permission. Later the king summoned his important ministers to come to his palace for a banquet. The banquet would take all day. The wives and ladies then saw that the elder had gone to the banquet, and so they decided to go to where the Buddha was. They kowtowed and did obeisance. They sat down for a while, listening to the scriptures, and each of them made a vow, saying: 'Let us never meet evil people! May we always meet with moral and noble people in our places of rebirth! We have heard that in the future there will be a Buddha called Śākyamuni. We wish to meet him, to go forth to apply ourselves to the Path, and to follow his instructions!'" The Buddha said to Ānanda: "The five hundred wives and ladies of that time are the present five hundred nuns. Because of the sincerity of their vow they now deserve to be saved. That is why the World-honored One saved them!" When the Buddha had explained this, there was none who was not glad.

Volume Two

Chapter XII

(continued)

Formerly, when the Buddha had just attained the Path, he was in the land of Rājagṛha. While making conversions he gradually arrived in the land of Śrāvastī. The king and his ministers all honored him. Then there was a merchant, an important person, called Po-li (Bhallika?). He went to sea with five hundred merchants searching for precious things. The spirit of the sea then came out. He held a handful of water and asked Po-li: "Is the water of the sea plenty or is my handful of water plenty?" Po-li answered: "The handful of water is plenty." "Why?" "The water of the sea may be plenty, but it is useless for one's present need. It cannot save a thirsty person. A handful of water may be little, but if one meets a thirsty person one may use it and give it to him to save his life. The merit one will experience in later times is incalculable." The spirit of the sea was glad, and he said in praise: "Excellent!" He then took off his eightfold fragrant necklace, comparable to the seven precious things, to present to Po-li. While the spirit of the sea accompanied him, he went back safely and arrived in the land of Śrāvastī. He presented the fragrant necklace to King Prasenajit and gave a complete account of its origin. "I think this fragrant necklace must not be worn by me. I respectfully offer it to you. I hope you will accept it." The king received the fragrant necklace and he thought it wonderful. So he called the women and had them line up in front of him. He would give the fragrant necklace to the most beautiful one. Sixty thousand women came in complete

585b

71

attire. The king asked: "Why did my wife Mallikā not come forward?" A servant answered: "Today is the fifteenth day. She observes the fast according to the Doctrine of the Buddha. She dresses in plain clothes, not in grand attire. That is why she does not come forward." Then the king became angry and he sent someone to call her, saying: "To observe the fast now, do you not disobey the king's orders?" When he had thus sent for her three times, Lady Mallikā came forward dressed in plain clothes. Among the multitude she was as bright as the sun and moon, and twice as beautiful as usual. The king was startled, and as his respect increased he said: "What virtue do you possess that you are so exceptionally bright?" The wife said to the king: "I think I have a little merit. I have received this female form. The impurity of its sensual nature night and day accumulates like a mountain. But one's life is short, and one is afraid of falling into the three woeful destinations. That is why I observe the fast of the Buddha's Doctrine in my life. If one stops craving and follows the Path, one will meet with merit in every existence." The king rejoiced upon hearing this, and he gave the fragrant necklace to his wife Mallikā. His wife replied: "I am observing the fast now. I cannot wear this! You may give it to someone else." The king said: "It was my intention to give it to the most excellent one. You are the most excellent now. Moreover, you observe the fast of the Doctrine, and your determination for the Path is extremely strong. Therefore I give it to you. If you do not accept it, I shall put it away." His wife replied: "Oh great king, do not be grieved! I hope that you, O king, will depart from your intention and go with me to where the Buddha is. Present this fragrant necklace to the World-honored One, and collect the noble teaching, thus accumulating a kalpa's (eon's) merit!" The king agreed with her. So he ordered a stately carriage and went to where the Buddha was. He kowtowed to the ground and withdrew to his royal seat. The king said to the Buddha: "The fragrant necklace of the spirit of the sea was presented to me by Po-li. Of sixty thousand wives, there was none who did not want to obtain it. I offered it to Mallikā, but she did not take it. She was observing the fast of the Buddha's Doctrine, and her mind did not covet it. I respectfully present it to you, O Buddha. I hope that you will deign to accept it. Your disciples, World-honored One, firmly keep their fast. Such is their honest faith! How meritorious!" Thereupon the World-honored One accepted the fragrant necklace and he spoke the stanzas:

5. If one uses many precious flowers, the hairdo will become beautiful. If one widely accumulates the fragrance of virtue, one's rebirth will change for the better. 585c

6. The scent of herbs and fragrant flowers does not go against the wind. [But] close to the Path and spreading widely, the scent of a virtuous one goes everywhere.

7. Regarding the fragrance of sandalwood and *tagara,* and the fragrant flower of the blue lotus, even though one may say: "This is genuine!", none could be compared to the scent of the precepts.

8. When the fragrance of a flower is weak, one must not call it genuine! But the scent of keeping the precepts reaches the gods and is most excellent.

9. When one embodies the precepts, and does not deviate in one's conduct, the mind becomes tranquil and is delivered, and one is thereby distanced free from Māra's path.

After the Buddha had expounded the stanzas, he again informed the king: "The fame of the merits of fasting reaches far and wide. When Lady Mallikā observes the fast of the Buddha's Doctrine for one day and one night, this is better than if, for instance, the sixteen great countries were filled with precious objects and one were to take them and give them away. If one compares the merits, it is like comparing Mount Sumeru and a single bean! If one accumulates merit and applies oneself to wisdom, one may attain nirvana." The king and his wife, and his ministers great and small, were all happy. They dedicated themselves to the practice of the Doctrine.

Once the Buddha was on Mount Gṛdhrakūṭa in Rājagṛha. In the city there were fifty sons of the elders. They went to where the Buddha was, did obeisance, withdrew, and sat down. The Buddha explained to them the Doctrine relative to impermanence, suffering, emptiness, and selflessness. "Affection is like a dream. Having come together, people will soon part. Although esteemed and honored, one still feels sorrow. Only in nirvana is one forever freed from the cycle of birth and death. When all misfortunes are completely appeased, one will be in absolute peace." Upon hearing the Doctrine, the fifty people were happy, and they wished to be his disciples. The Buddha said: "Welcome, monks!" Their hair fell off of itself and they donned the robe of the Doctrine to become ascetics. These ascetics had relatives and friends who were elders. When the elders heard that they had gone forth, they were very happy for them. They went to Mount Gṛdhrakūṭa to meet them, and said in praise of them: "You were eager to obtain fine gain, and now you have the determination!" They set up an altar for them and invited the Buddha and his Sangha. The next day the Buddha and his Sangha came to the dwelling to eat. After the meal, he expounded the Doctrine, and they departed in the afternoon. Those ascetics who had recently become adepts hankered after their kin and wanted to revert back to mundane life. The Buddha knew what was on their minds. As he was about to leave through the gates of the city, he saw that in the foul mud, covered by night soil in the ditch of a field, there grew lotus flowers. They were colorful and their scent was clear. Their scent was so fragrant that it overwhelmed any stench. So the Buddha quickly went back to them and spoke the stanzas:

586a
    10. Just as in a [filthy] ditch in the field near a major road, there grows a lotus flower with a clear delightful scent,

    11. The same applies to the cycle of birth and death. The mundane person remains in the cycle, but the wise one takes leave of it as a [true] disciple of the Buddha.

Having spoken the stanzas, the Buddha returned to the mountain. The worthy Ānanda came forward and said to the Buddha: "When you were near the ditch in the field, World-honored One, I did not understand the meaning of the two stanzas you proclaimed there. I would like to hear what they mean." The Buddha informed Ānanda: "Did you see that in the impurity of foul mud, on the night soil in the ditch, there grew lotus flowers?" "Yes, I saw them." The Buddha said: "Ānanda, when man is in the world he proceeds from birth to birth. Considering a life of a hundred years, more or less, one goes through love for wife and child, hunger and thirst, cold and warmth, sadness or happiness. Moreover, there are one misfortune, two good fortunes, the three poisons, the four errors, the five aggregates, the six entrances, the seven consciousnesses, the eight wrongs, the nine vexations, and the ten evils to contend with. They are all like the impurity of foul mud, the night soil accumulated in the ditch in the field. All of a sudden there comes a person who realizes that the world is impermanent, who is intent on applying himself to the Path, develops his determination for purity, concentrates his spirit, destroys false notions, and ultimately brings about his attainment of the Path. He is like a lovely lotus flower that grows in foul mud. He by himself attains the Path, and saves his kin as well. All beings will open up in full understanding. He is also like the scent of a flower that overwhelms the stench." When the fifty monks had heard the Buddha's exposition of the Doctrine, their determination became firmer and they attained arhatship.

Chapter XIII

The Fool

Once the Buddha was in the land of Śrāvastī. At that time there was a brahman in the city who was going on eighty years and whose wealth was immeasurable. As a person he was foolish and niggardly, and very difficult to convert. He was not aware of the virtue of the Path, nor did he understand the nature of impermanence. But he still built a fine dwelling: a room at the front and a hall in the back, a cool terrace and a warm room, tens of spans of side rooms to the east and the west. Only the sunshades in front of the rear hall were not yet completed. The brahman always managed and directed everything by himself. The Buddha saw with his eyes of the Path that this old man's life would not last all day and that he would go to the nether world. He could not know that himself, and he was simply too busy with his preparations anyway. His spirit did not have any merit. He was really in a pitiable condition. The Buddha led Ānanda to his gate. He asked the old man how he felt. "Are you not too tired? This dwelling you are building now, for what purpose is it?" The old man said: "In the front room I shall welcome visitors and in the hall in the back I shall dwell by myself. In the side rooms both east and west I shall have my children, my possessions, and servants. In summer I shall mount my cool terrace and in winter I shall go to my warm room." The Buddha said to the old man: "For a long time I have heard about you, aged virtuous one. I thought of postponing our conversation, but I happen to have important stanzas. Alive or dead, they are beneficial. I would like to give them to you as a present. I wonder if you could just put your things aside for a while and sit   586b

77

down with me to discuss them?" The old man answered: "Right now I am very busy. I cannot afford to sit down to talk. Come again at a later day and I shall have a good chat with you. The important stanzas you mention, you can expound them now." Thereupon the World-honored One spoke the stanzas:

1. "I have a son. I have riches," the fool ponders anxiously, but he is not himself. Why is he concerned about a son and riches!

2. "In summer I shall stay here. In winter I shall stay there." A fool often ponders in advance, but he does not know about the upcoming turn of events.

3. A fool's foolishness goes to the extreme when he says that he is wise. When a fool confidently calls himself wise, he is called an utter fool.

The brahman said: "You have spoken these stanzas well. You are really keeping me up now! Come later and we shall discuss them again!" The Buddha was grieved then, and he left. Later on the old man walked under a rafter which fell and hit his head. His life was lost immediately. His family wept, and it shocked his four neighbors. The Buddha had not yet gone far when this mishap took place. When the Buddha returned to the village, he met tens of brahmans. They asked the Buddha where he had come from and the Buddha said: "Earlier, when I arrived at the house of the deceased old man, I expounded the Doctrine to him, but he did not believe in the Buddha's words. He was ignorant of his own impermanence. Now he has all of a sudden gone to the nether world." He again fully explained the meaning of the previous stanzas to the brahmans. Upon hearing them they were delighted, and attained the Path. Thereupon the World-honored One spoke the stanzas:

4. A fool approaches a wise one just like a ladle that scoops something flavorful. Even if he associates with the wise for a long time, he still does not know the Doctrine.

5. An intelligent person approaches a wise one just like a tongue that tastes something flavorful. Even though he associates with the wise for just a while, he immediately understands the essence of the Path.

6. When a fool acts, he brings calamity on himself. He readily performs evil, bringing grave misfortune on himself.

7. If one's action is not wholesome, afterward one feels remorse. It brings on a tearful countenance. The retribution comes from one's previous practice.

Then, when the brahmans had heard these stanzas, they increased their sincere faith. They did obeisance to the Buddha, were delighted, and carried out their dedicated practice.

Once the Buddha was in the pure abode of Anāthapiṇḍada in the land of Śrāvastī, expounding the Doctrine to gods and men. At that time King Prasenajit had a widowed daughter called Vajrā (Vajrakumārī). She had returned as a young widow. Her father, the king, felt sorry for her and constructed a separate palace for her elegant livelihood. He gave her five hundred singing girls to amuse her. Among them was an elderly servant, called Kubjottarā, who used to go to the market to buy ointments and powder, incense, and flowers. Once she saw a huge crowd of men and women leave town, each holding incense and flowers. So she asked them: "Where are you going?" The crowd replied: "The Buddha has appeared in this existence, the most revered one in the three worlds. He will deliver all beings [from suffering] and all will obtain nirvana." When Kubjottarā heard this, she was delighted and full of joy. So she thought to herself: "That I meet the Buddha now in my old age is a merit of my previous existence." She immediately took part of the incense money to buy beautiful flowers. She followed the crowd and went to where the Buddha was. She did obeisance, stepped aside, scattered the flowers, and burned the incense, and then listened attentively to the Doctrine. After she had left the

586c

market, she handled some incense. But on account of listening to the Doctrine and pursued by her previous behavior, the scent of the incense was sweeter and its weight twice as heavy. [Her employers] did not like her being late and they all reproached her. As a loyal servant Kubjottarā stated the facts: "In this existence there is a noble teacher, the most honored one in the three worlds. When he beats the unsurpassed drum of the Doctrine, it reverberates throughout the trichiliocosmos. Those who went to listen to his Doctrine were countless. Truly, I followed and listened to his Doctrine. That is why I was delayed." When the followers of Vajrā heard her explanation that the meaning of the Doctrine of the World-honored One was very profound, unheard of in this world, they were delighted and joyful, and they sighed: "What did we do wrong that we alone did not hear it?" So they asked Kubjottarā to expound it to them. Kubjottarā said: "I am a lowly person and my words are unclear. I do not dare to expound it. I beg you to [send me to] seek his advice again, and I shall explain it according to his command." They immediately sent her out and told her again: "Communicate to us the complete proceedings!" When Kubjottarā had yet to return, the servants of Vajrā were in the courtyard, restless as a child waiting for his mother. The Buddha informed Kubjottarā: "If you go back and expound the Doctrine, many will be saved. As for the right deportment when expounding the Doctrine, first set up a high seat!" When Kubjottarā had received the instructions, she reported in full the noble command, and they were all very delighted. They took off their garments, and piled them up to form a high seat. When Kubjottarā had cleansed herself, she received the Buddha's majestic power and expounded the Doctrine as empowered. Vajrā and the others, more than five hundred people, had their doubts resolved. They destroyed their evil and attained the path of stream-enterer. The exposition of the Doctrine was so beautiful that they were not aware of being consumed by fire. In one moment they burned to death and were reborn in heaven. The king led his attendants to rescue them from the fire, but when he saw that they were burned, he prepared the coffins and shrouds. After the burial he went to where the Buddha was. He did obeisance to the Buddha, withdrew, and sat down on his usual throne. The Buddha asked the king where he came from. The king brought his hands together and said: "My daughter Vajrā was so unfortunate as to catch fire unexpectedly. Everything was completely burned. I am just back from [seeing] her coffin and shroud. I wonder what she did wrong that she was destroyed by fire? Please, World-honored One, tell me about that unknown [event]." The Buddha informed the great king: "In the past there 587a was a city called Benares. There was an elder's wife who led five hundred ladies out of the city to conduct a large sacrifice. The rule was that it was not to be tolerated that someone from another family came near. No matter whether close or distant, those who came were thrown into the fire. There was an aspirant for Buddha-hood [*pratyekabuddha*] in the world then, called Kāla. He lived in the mountains. In the morning he came begging for alms and in the evening he quickly returned to the mountains. Kāla came upon the sacrifice on his begging rounds. When the elder's wife saw him, she was furious. They all grasped him and pushed him into the fire. When his whole body was ablaze, he used his supernatural power and flew up in the air. The women were terrified and repented their misdeed in tears. They knelt deeply, raised their heads and stated: 'We women were foolish, ignorant of your utter truthfulness. We fools were so deranged as to disgrace your divine spirit. When considering our wrongdoing, the crime is as huge as a mountain. Please descend, respected Venerable, so we may do away with our serious misfortune!' Immediately after these words, he came down and entered *parinirvāṇa*. The women erected a stupa and worshiped his relics." The Buddha expounded to the great king the stanzas:

8. When a fool commits evil, he cannot understand it. He will burn, pursued by misfortune, and his misdeed will turn into a blazing fire.

9. As for the place a fool is looking forward to, he does not think he will have any suffering. But when he is about to fall into a place of distress, then he knows [belatedly] it is not good.

The Buddha informed the great king: "The elder's wife at the time is your present daughter Vajrā. The five hundred servants are the present five hundred singing girls, including Kubjottarā. Merit and demerit pursue a person. They do not remain unmanifested for long. Good and evil follow a person, just as the shadow follows the form." When he had proclaimed this Doctrine, the mighty and lowly in the land devoutly subjected themselves. They were all glad and took refuge in the Buddha, Dharma, and Sangha. They all accepted the five precepts and attained the Path.

Chapter XIV

The Wise Man

There once was a brahman who was twenty years old. He was a natural genius. When something, no matter how big or small, passed before his eyes, he knew it. He thought he was clever and made a vow: "The skills of the world, I shall know them all! If there is one skill that I cannot master, then I am not intelligent." Thereupon he set out to study. There was no teacher he did not seek out. Adept at the various methods of the six arts, astronomy, geography, healing through medicine, landslides and earthquakes, playing dice and chess, playing of artful music, cutting out garments, embroidering silk, slicing prepared viands, and blending flavors, he was equally versed in human affairs. He thought to himself: "None can compete with me! I shall put myself to the test traveling through the countries and I shall overcome any opposition. My name will spread over the four seas and my expertise will hit the sky. Then they will record my achievements on bamboo and silk, and my merits will be handed down for a hundred generations." Thereupon he set out on his way and arrived in a country. Entering the marketplace, he looked around and saw a man   587b sitting down and making a bow out of a horn. While he was separating the strings and fashioning the horn, his hands looked as if they were flying. His adjustments were swift as he made the bow. The buyers pressed around him, vying with each other. So he thought to himself: "Since my youth I have thought that my learning was complete. I did not anticipate feeling inadequate for not learning to make a bow. If I were to contest his skill, I would lose! I must learn from him!" So he followed the bow-maker and sought to be his disciple. He received the learning with heart and soul, and in time he gained complete understanding of the way of the bow. His art was so ingenious that he even surpassed his teacher. He then gave away his possessions, took his leave, and went away.

While on his way to another country, he had to ford a river. There was a boatman who was handling his boat as if he were flying. He was turning, going up and down with incomparable swiftness. Again he thought to himself: "My skills may be numerous, but I have never gained experience with a boat. It may be a humble skill, but I do not know it and I should learn it and be equipped with all ten thousand skills." So he followed the boatman and sought to be his disciple. He accorded him the utmost respect and toiled with all his might. In time he knew what was right or wrong. He was making turns while managing the boat far better than his teacher. He then gave away his possessions, took his leave, and went away.

Again he reached another country. The king's palace was beyond compare in the world. So he thought to himself: "The carpenter who built this palace—how skillful he is! All the while I have been traveling in anonymity, I somehow did not learn this. If I were to compete against his skill, I certainly would not win! I must again apply myself, so that my mind will be satisfied!" So he sought out the carpenter and wished to be his disciple. He honored him with all his heart and took up the ax. In time he gained complete understanding of the measurements, of square and round, of compass and square. He knew completely the [details of] timberwork, the carved designs, and the inlay work. His natural genius was evident and his work instantly surpassed that of his teacher. He then gave away his possessions, took leave from his teacher, and went away.

He roamed around the world, through all sixteen great countries. He overcame his opponents and mastered their skills. Every single word and every single step, there was none who ventured to respond. He was arrogant and said: "Who could excel me under heaven and on earth?" When the Buddha was in the Jetavana, he

saw from afar that this man deserved to be saved. With his supernatural power the Buddha transformed himself into an ascetic.
Leaning on a staff and holding his alms bowl, he came right up to
him. In the land where the brahman came from, there was no
Doctrine of the Path. He had not yet seen an ascetic and wondered
who this man was. He would ask him at the right moment. In a
little while the ascetic had arrived and the brahman asked: "I have
not yet seen anyone like you according to the rules of a hundred
kings. Your garments do not exist in the regulations for clothing.
One does not see these implements among the different objects in
ancestral temples. What kind of a person are you that your appearance and clothes are so unusual?" The ascetic replied: "I am
someone who manages himself." He again asked: "What do you
mean by managing yourself?" Thereupon the ascetic relied on what
[the brahman] had practiced and he spoke the stanzas:

1. A bow-maker manages the horn and a boatman manages his boat. The skillful carpenter manages the wood
and a wise one manages himself.

2. Like a large rock that cannot be moved by the wind, a
wise one's mind is grave. He is not moved by slander or
praise.

3. Just as a deep pool is still and pure, the wise one learns
the Path and his mind is pure and joyful.

When the ascetic had spoken these stanzas, he ascended into the
sky and manifested himself as the Buddha. The brightness of his
thirty-two marks and eighty secondary marks was pervasive and
illuminated heaven and earth. He descended from the sky and
said to that man: "The quality of the Path gives me the strength
to transform and manage myself." Thereupon the man fell prostrate in obeisance, kowtowed, and asked: "I wish to hear what is
most important when managing oneself!" The Buddha informed
the brahman: "The five precepts, the ten wholesome [paths of ac-
tion], the four immeasurables, the six perfections, the four trances,

587c

and the three deliverances: these are the methods of managing oneself. The wonderful skills of the six arts, of the bow-maker, the boatman, and the carpenter, these are all beautiful adornments [but are also] elements of specious fame. An unsettled personality and a lax mind lead the way to [repeated] birth and death." Upon hearing this the brahman was joyful, and gained true understanding. He wished to be his disciple, and the Buddha informed him: "Welcome, ascetic!" His hair fell off of itself and he became an ascetic. The Buddha explained to him the essence of the four noble truths and the eight deliverances. He subsequently attained the path of arhatship.

Once the Buddha was in the land of Śrāvastī. Five hundred *li* from the land there was a village of fifty or sixty families in the mountains. A poor family lived in the village. The mother was pregnant, and in the tenth month she gave birth to twin boys. They were beautiful beyond compare. Their parents loved them and they gave them names. One was called Shuang-te and the other Shuang-fu. Fifty or sixty days after their birth, their father had been pasturing the cows and returned home worn out. He withdrew and lay down on his bed. Their mother had left for the field to gather firewood and had not returned. The two small boys looked around but did not see their parents. They then both started talking in a reproving manner. One said: "In a previous existence we were about to obtain the Path, but we were correctly punished for our foolish notion that life is permanent. We fell back into the cycle of birth and death for countless eons. Now we are born as sons in this poor family. We cover ourselves with rough blankets in the straw. Our food and drink are coarse. We barely sustain ourselves. If it remains like this for a long time, how can we stay alive! We are being punished for our longing for riches and honor in a previous life, for letting ourselves go, and for spending some thought about momentary happiness. Ever since then we have been experiencing suffering on our long journey. We feel sorrow now, but what can we resort to?" The other answered: "We were young then. The diligence of one moment was not vigorously pursued, after all, and this made us meet with painful calamities in several existences. This is our own doing. It is not caused by our parents. We shall just have to face it together. What else is there to say?" The father heard his two sons making such reproaches, and he was very surprised. "Ah, they must be evil spirits that have come to bring disaster. How can small children only several tens of days old say such words? I am afraid that they will later kill their parents and destroy the family. I must kill them while they are still very young, 588a not yet grown up." The father left in a state of fright. He shut the door and went to the fields to gather firewood. He wanted to start a fire to burn them to death. The mother was on her way back and she asked her husband what the firewood was for. The husband said: "Very weird! Such were the nature of their words. They were like demons, out to destroy their own family. I want to burn them to death while they are still young." When the mother heard this, she was disconcerted. She was doubtful and did not believe it [and she said,] "It would be better to wait for a few days and listen together to what they are saying." For a few days, she tried to listen to their talk. Subsequently, when husband and wife were leaving by the door, they overheard their sons inside making reproaches as before. When the husband and wife heard this again, they thought it very weird. And so they piled up firewood with the secret wish to burn them.

The Buddha saw with his divine eye that the husband and wife wanted to burn their two children to death. He felt grieved. They were pitiable, but [he knew that] their former merits would save them. He went to their village, his luminous light shining everywhere. Heaven and earth moved greatly, and mountains, rivers, and trees were all gold-colored. Great and small in the village were startled and went to where the Buddha was. They did obeisance to the Buddha and there was none who was not glad. They knew that the Buddha was the highest spirit, unequaled in the three worlds. The Buddha arrived at the house of the twin children. When the two children saw the Buddha's light, their joy was unbounded. The parents were startled too, and they each carried one child to where the Buddha was. They asked the Buddha, the World-honored One: "Forty or fifty days after these children were born, they spoke wicked words. We thought it very uncanny. We feared they may cause harm. We wanted to burn them to death. As you just happened to come, O Buddha, they are yet not burned. We do not know what kind of demons these children are. We just wish that you would explain what sort of pernicious demons they are." When the children saw the Buddha, they were in rapturous delight. When the Buddha saw the children, he laughed heartily. From his mouth came a five-colored light, illuminating the whole of heaven and earth. The Buddha informed the parents of the children, and also the young and old of the village: "These two children are no demons but meritorious children. Formerly, at the time of the Buddha Kāśyapa, they used to be ascetics. They had been friends and comrades as youngsters, and when they had gone forth each was zealous. When they were about to obtain the Path, a heterodox notion suddenly came up and they were checked, content with worldly splendor. Because of their merits, however, they were reborn in heaven, and they descended as kings, as lords, and as elders, but when this [worldly] notion had suddenly arisen, they fell further and regressed. They did not obtain nirvana but experienced the cycle of birth and death. They were constantly dragged through a successive number of eons, and they were suddenly reborn as twins. They have just now been reborn in my time. Because they have worshiped the Buddha ever since, they deserve salvation because of their remaining merits. Through the extinction of their evil and the rise of their merit, they are conscious of their previous lives. So I, the World-honored One, have deliberately come to save them. If I did not save them, they would unreasonably be burned by fire." Thereupon the World-honored One spoke the stanzas:

> 4. Superior persons are physically without desire. They
> shine brightly wherever they are. Even though they may

experience suffering or happiness, they manifest wisdom without pride.

5. A wise superior person does not have worldly posses- sions. He does not aspire for son, wealth, or country. He constantly guards the path of moral conduct and wisdom, and does not covet false riches and honor.

6. A wise person knows that excitement is like a tree in the sand. When a friend's resolve is not yet strong, one follows beauty, tainted by its essence.

When the Buddha had expounded this, the children saw the Buddha and immediately jumped up with joy, just as eight-year-old children do. They became ascetics and attained arhatship. When the villagers young and old had seen the Buddha's radiant appearance and had also seen that the children's appearance had changed, their joy was great and they attained the path of the stream-enterer. The doubts of the parents were lifted and they also obtained the eye of the Doctrine.

Chapter XV

The Arhat

Once there was a country, called Nādika, in the vicinity of the Southern Sea. The people's normal occupation was gathering pearls and sandalwood. In that country there was a family with two brothers. Their parents had died and they wanted to divide the possessions. In the family there was a slave called Pūrṇa. He was young and intelligent. In trade and business, or making a living by going to sea, there was nothing he did not know. The residence and the possessions were considered one part and the slave Pūrṇa as the other part. The brothers then cast lots and the younger brother obtained Pūrṇa. He took his wife and children and left the house empty-handed. There was scarcity in the world at that time. Possessing only Pūrṇa, he was afraid they would not make ends meet and was very sad. The slave Pūrṇa said to his master: "Please do not be sad! I, Pūrṇa, will deliberate on something, and within months I shall make you surpass your brother." The master said: "If you can definitely achieve this, I shall set you free as a worthy person." The wife of the master had some pearls and other things, and gave them to Pūrṇa as his capital. Then, when the tide came in, the people in the city went to the shores to gather firewood. Pūrṇa took some pearls and other things and left the city. He saw a mendicant carrying firewood on his back. In the firewood there was the fragrance of *gośīrṣa* sandalwood. It could cure serious illnesses. One ounce was worth a thousand taels of gold. One could not always obtain it in the world at that time. Pūrṇa knew this. He bought it for two coins, took it home, and divided it into ten. There was an elder then who had contracted a serious illness. He

91

had to have two ounces of this fragrant *gosīrṣa* sandalwood as his medicine. He had sought for it for a long while but could not obtain it. Pūrṇa took it to him and got two thousand taels of gold. When he had sold everything in this way, the wealth he had accumulated was ten times greater than the older brother's. The master was grateful for Pūrṇa's kindness. He did not break his word and set him free as a worthy person, to enjoy himself as he pleased.

Thereupon Pūrṇa bade farewell and applied himself to the Path. He went to the land of Śrāvastī, did obeisance to the Buddha, knelt deeply, and said to the Buddha: "The place I came from is insignificant, but I find happiness in the qualities of the Path. I hope that you, World-honored One, will show me your kindness and save me." The Buddha said: "Welcome, Pūrṇa!" His hair fell off of itself. The robe of the Doctrine covered him, and he became an ascetic. The Buddha expounded the Doctrine to him, and he subsequently attained arhatship. He sat down and thought to himself: "I now have the six superknowledges and the freedom of life or ruin, and all this because of my master's kindness. Now I must go to save him and convert my countrymen." Thereupon, Pūrṇa went back to his country, to the house of his master. His master was very happy, invited him to sit down, and arranged for a meal. After the meal he washed his hands and flew up in the sky. He divided himself by splitting his body. From the halves gushed out water and fire. His brightness was penetrating. He came down from on high and informed his master: "These supernatural qualities all came from the merit of your setting me free. I went to where the Buddha was, and such was what I have learned." The master answered: "The Buddha's spiritual conversion is so fine! I would like to meet the World-honored One and receive his teaching." Pūrṇa replied: "Just wholeheartedly provide for food vessels. The Buddha has the three penetrating insights. He will certainly come himself." He then immediately made the provisions. Having made the customary arrangements, he kowtowed toward the land of Śrāvastī and knelt deeply. He burned incense and invited the Buddha: "I hope that you will condescend generously to save us

588c

92

all!" The Buddha knew his intentions, and so he went with his five hundred arhats, each with his magic power, to his house. The king and his people were all respectful. He came to where the Buddha was and fell prostrate in obeisance. He withdrew and sat down on his royal seat. When he had cleansed himself after the meal, the Buddha extensively explained his bright Doctrine to the master and to the king and his assembled officials. They all accepted the five precepts and became the Buddha's disciples. They rose, stood in front of the Buddha, and praised Pūrṇa: "You were diligent as a layman, and having gone forth you obtained the Path. Your supernatural qualities are so lofty and far-reaching that our family and country have been saved. How shall we recompense your kindness!" Thereupon, the World-honored One praised Pūrṇa and spoke the stanzas:

1. When one's thoughts are calm, when one's verbal behavior has ceased, and when one is delivered through what is right, one is at rest with everything extinguished.

2. When one has discarded desire and is without attachment, when one has done away with the hindrance of the three realms, and when all aspirations have ceased, one is said to be a superior man.

3. In a village or in the wilds, on level ground or on a high shore, wherever an arhat has passed there is none who is not saved.

4. They [arhats] find happiness in seclusion, but common people do not. Delightfully without aspirations, they do not long for anything.

After the Buddha had spoken the stanzas, the master and the king increased their joy. They worshiped for seven days and attained the path of the stream-enterer.

Chapter XVI

An Account of Thousands

Once the Buddha was in the land of Śrāvastī. There was an aged monk called Panthaka who had only recently become a monk. He was ignorant by nature, and so the Buddha had five hundred arhats instruct him daily. In three years he still did not achieve understanding of even a single stanza. The four classes [of people] in the land all knew that he was ignorant. The Buddha had pity on him, and so he called him and gave him the following stanza: "Guard your mouth and control your mind! The body must not commit anything wrong! He who behaves thus can be delivered from the world." Panthaka was moved by the Buddha's kindness. He was glad, his mind opened up, and he was able to recite the stanza. The Buddha informed him: "Your age may now be advanced; you have achieved reciting the stanza. Everyone knows it. One must not think of it as odd. I shall now explain its meaning to you. Listen well and with all your heart!" As Panthaka listened to the teaching, the Buddha explained to him that the body is the basis for the three [good actions], the mouth for four, and the mind for three. He explained about the contemplation of their origin and their extinction, and that one ceaselessly revolves in the five destinations and the three realms. Because of this, one either ascends to heaven or falls into the abyss, but also because of this one attains the Path and nirvana comes naturally. He distinctly explained immeasurable wonderful things to him. Panthaka's mind suddenly opened up and he attained arhatship.

At that time there were five hundred nuns living in a separate pure abode. Daily the Buddha sent a monk to expound the scriptural Doctrine. One day it was Panthaka's turn to go. When the nuns heard this, they all chuckled in anticipation: "When he comes tomorrow, we shall say the stanza backwards and make him ashamed and speechless." When Panthaka went to the nuns' abode the next day, they all came forward, young and old, did obeisance, looked at each other, and laughed. When he sat down they gave him food, and after the meal he washed his hands and they invited him to expound the Doctrine. Panthaka then mounted his high seat and self-deprecatingly said: "With few qualities and inferior talent I finally became an ascetic. I have been obtuse for quite a while. What I have learned is not much. I only know one stanza. I roughly know its meaning. I shall extend its knowledge to you. Please, may you each listen quietly!" When the young nuns wanted to say the stanza backwards, they could not open their mouths. They were frightened and reproved themselves. They kowtowed and repented their wrongdoing. Panthaka then one by one distinguished the elements, just as the Buddha had explained: the bases of body and mind, evil and merit, internal and external, the ascent to heaven and the obtaining of the Path, concentration of the spirit, annihilation of notions, and entering into concentration. When the nuns heard his explanation, they thought immediately it was peculiarly uncanny. They were wholeheartedly glad and they all entered the path of the arhat.

Later, Prasenajit, the king of the land, invited the Buddha and his congregation for an assembly in his main hall. Wishing to demonstrate Panthaka's imposing spirit, the Buddha gave him his alms bowl to carry, and he followed behind. The doorkeeper recognized him and detained him. He did not allow him to enter. "You are an ascetic who does not understand a single stanza. Why would you be invited! I am a layman and yet I know the stanzas! How much more should an ascetic, but you are without knowledge! There is no point in being charitable toward you. You cannot enter." So Panthaka remained outside the gate while the Buddha sat down in the hall. When they had passed the water, Panthaka took the bowl, stretched his arms, and handed it from afar to the Buddha. The king, his ministers, his wife, the crown prince, and the four classes of the congregation saw the arms coming in, but they did not see the body. In amazement they asked the Buddha whose arms they were. The Buddha said: "They are the arms of the monk Panthaka. He recently attained the Path. I let him take my bowl earlier, but the doorkeeper did not allow him to enter. That is why he stretches his arms, and gives me my bowl!" They immediately invited him in. His spirit was twice as imposing as usual. The king said to the Buddha: "I have heard that Panthaka is by nature ignorant. He just knows one stanza. Why did he attain the Path?" The Buddha informed the king: "Learning is not great; practice is superior. Panthaka understands the meaning of one stanza. Its purity of reason has entered his spirit. His body, mouth, and mind are calm, pure as celestial gold. Someone may have studied much, but if he does not understand and practice it, he merely ruins his consciousness. What is the advantage?" Thereupon the World-honored One spoke the stanzas:

1. Although one is capable of reciting a thousand stanzas and has incorrect understanding of them, it would be better to learn one important thing which extinguishes evil thoughts!

2. Although one is capable of speaking a thousand words, what is the advantage if they are meaningless? It would be better to learn a single meaningful thing so as to practice and be delivered.

3. Although one may often recite the scriptural texts, what is the advantage if one does not understand them? If one understands one verse of the Doctrine and practices it, one may attain the Path.

After the Buddha had spoken the stanzas, two hundred monks attained arhatship. The king, his ministers, his wife, and the crown prince were all very happy.

Once the Buddha was in the land of Śrāvastī, in a pure abode, and expounded the Doctrine to gods and men. Then there was a brahman in that land, an elder by the name of Rāmadatta. He

had limitless wealth. The possessions of his family were immeasurable. According to the rules of the brahman class, one must display extensive largesse in order to show one's fame. Dispensing the family riches, he used them as gifts. Arranging for the *pañcavārṣika* (the five-yearly entertainment of the Order), he established worship to more than five thousand brahmans. In five years he had offered clothing, bedding, medicine, rare precious objects, and implements for the sacrifices, all highly coveted things. For the elder Rāmadatta the brahmans conducted sacrifices during the five years to the gods, the four mountains, the five sacred peaks, the constellations, water, and fire. There was nothing that was not complete. They made incantations asking that the elder would experience prosperity for a long time. When the five years were over, on the very last day he was most generous, following the rules of the elders. Golden bowls were filled with silver grain and silver bowls were filled with golden wheat. Elephants and horses, carriages, servants, valuables, personal adornments of the seven precious things, parasols, shoes, deerskin clothes, staffs, couches, washing pitchers and vessels, beds and sleeping mats, everything they had to have, eighty-four thousand things, he gave them all. On that very day they all came to the great gathering. Spiritual beings, the king of the land, high officials, brahmans, and noted families all came to the gathering. In the hustle and
589c bustle there was none who was not glad. When the Buddha saw this, he sighed: "Why is this brahman of noted family so foolish! His gifts are great, but the meritorious recompense is small. It is like sowing seeds in fire; what benefit can one obtain! If I do not transform myself, he will be barred from entering the Doctrine for a long time." Thereupon the World-honored One rose and arranged his clothes in a dignified way. He transformed himself and emerged from the earth, emitting a very bright light that shone all over the gathered multitude. Young and old were surprised at this wondrous sight. They were startled and terrified, not knowing what the spirit was. The elder Rāmadatta and the whole multitude touched the ground with their heads and did obeisance to the

Buddha. The Buddha saw that everyone in the crowd had respectful minds, and because of their reverential demeanor he then spoke the stanzas:

> 4. Every month one may perform a thousand sacrifices uninterruptedly throughout one's entire life, but it is better to be mindful of the Doctrine for a single moment. The merits one brings about in one such moment are superior to those of an entire life.

> 5. Although during the hundred years of one's lifetime, one may serve the god of fire, it is better to worship the Buddha, Dharma, and Sangha for a single moment. The merits of one moment of homage are superior to those of a hundred years.

Thereupon the World-honored One informed Rāmadatta: "Giving is fourfold. What are the four? First, although one gives much, the meritorious recompense one obtains is small. Second, although one gives little, the meritorious recompense one obtains is great. Third, one gives much and the meritorious recompense one obtains is also great. Fourth, one gives little and the meritorious recompense one obtains is also small.

"What is meant by, one gives much and the meritorious recompense one obtains is small? It is when a person is foolish and makes sacrifices by killing living beings, when he drinks spirits and sings and dances, when he dissipates his wealth and does not have meritorious wisdom. What is meant by, one gives little and the recompense one obtains is small? When one gives scantily and with evil intention to a man of the Path. Both are foolish and therefore have no merits. What is meant by, one gives little and the merits one obtains are great? When one can serve a moral person with kindness. After the man of the Path has eaten, one strenuously applies oneself to recitation. For one who does this, even though it is little, his merits are very great. What is meant by, one gives much and the merits one obtains are great? When there is a sage who knows that the world is impermanent, one gladly spends his wealth to construct a pure abode and an orchard. One brings worship to the Buddha, Dharma, and Sangha with clothes, bedding, and delicacies. These merits are like the five rivers streaming into the great ocean. Such is the flow of the merits, uninterrupted in every world. So when one gives much, the recompense is even greater. When for instance a farmer's soil is rich or poor, what he gets as a yield is not the same." At that moment, when the elder Rāmadatta and the people gathered there had seen the Buddha's transformation and when they had heard his exposition of the words of the Doctrine, they were all very glad. All gods, 590a people, and spirits attained the way of a stream-enterer. The five thousand brahmans all became ascetics and attained arhatship. Young and old who lived in the house of their master Rāmadatta accepted the five precepts and also attained the Path. The king of the land and his high officials all accepted the precepts and took refuge [in the Buddha, Dharma, and Sangha]. They became lay disciples (upāsakas) and attained the eye of the Doctrine.

Once, when the Buddha was in a pure abode in Śrāvastī teaching, there was a man in the land of Rājagṛha who was terribly foolish. He was not pious toward his parents, he was rude to the good, and he was disrespectful toward his elders. As his house was in decay and things never went according to his wishes, he took to serving the fire in the hope of gaining good fortune. As for his way of serving the fire, just when the sun would go down he would light a large pyre. He knelt and did obeisance towards it sometimes until late at night. When the fire was extinguished, he stopped. He acted in this way for three years, but he did not gain any good fortune. He further served the sun and moon. As for his way of serving the sun and moon, in the daytime when the sun had risen and at night when the moon was bright, he did obeisance, respectively, toward the sun and the moon. When they had gone down, he stopped. He acted in this way for three years, but he again did not gain any good fortune. He then served the gods. He burned incense, knelt, and did obeisance. He offered fine fragrant flowers, spirits and dried meats, pigs and sheep, cows and calves. Consequently he became poor and thus did not obtain good fortune. He was distressed and downcast. He fell ill and did not leave his house. He heard that in the land of Śrāvastī there was a Buddha honored by all gods. "I must go and serve him, and I certainly expect to obtain good fortune." So he went to where the Buddha was. When he reached the gate of the pure abode and looked up to the World-honored One, the Buddha's bright appearance was dazzling and his looks were extraordinary, just like the moon among the stars. Seeing the Buddha he was glad. He kowtowed, folded his hands, and said to the Buddha: "I have grown in foolishness, not aware of the Buddha, Dharma, and Sangha. I have served the fire, the sun and moon, and also the various gods. I have been zealous for nine years, but I have not received any good fortune. I am in distress and my strength declines. My four elements are often ailing, and I shall die shortly. I heard, World-honored One, that you are a teacher who saves others. That is why I have come from afar to seek refuge, wishing to be saved with good fortune." The Buddha informed him: "What you have served are all sorcery, bogeymen, and sprites. Your prayers and sacrifices are like a mountain, but your misdeeds are like the rivers and the sea. If you seek good fortune by killing living beings, you are far from good fortune! It just makes you suffer a hundred eons, without others' respect. When one prays and sacrifices using the pigs and sheep of the whole world, the misdeed is like Mount Sumeru, and there is not even an iota of good fortune. How would you not be affected by knowing that your expenditures have been in vain! Furthermore, you have not been pious toward your parents. You have treated the worthy with unconcern, and you have no respect for your elders. You are proud and haughty, and your three poisons abound. As your wrongs become more serious every day, why would you obtain merit? If you are capable of a change of heart, if you treat the worthy with respect, if your demeanor is dignified and reverential, if you serve your elders, if you reject evil and believe in good, and if you develop yourself and exalt kindness, four merits will increase day by day and you will never be ailing. What are the four? One, your appearance will be proper. Two, your strength will be strong. Three, you will be safe and without illness. Four, you will add years to your life and your end will not be untimely. If you practice unremittingly, you may obtain the Path too." Thereupon the World-honored One spoke the stanzas:

590b

6. When someone sacrifices to the spirits in order to seek merit and later anticipates a reward, he cannot expect even one of the four merits. It is better to pay homage to the worthy.

7. If your practice is truly reverential and always respectful of your elders, the four merits will naturally take effect: appearance, strength, longevity, and happiness.

When that man had heard these stanzas of the Buddha, he was very glad and gained pious understanding. He kowtowed and did obeisance. He again said to the Buddha: "Covered by the impurity of my misdeeds I have accumulated evil for nine years, but I was fortunate to be converted by kindness. Now I have achieved understanding. I do wish that you, World-honored One, will let me be an ascetic." The Buddha said, "Welcome, monk." His hair fell off of itself and he became an ascetic. He internally reflected on *ānāpāna* (breath counting) and attained arhatship.

Chapter XVII

Evil Conduct

Once the Buddha was in the land of Rājagṛha. He sent an arhat called Sumana to the south of Kaśmīr with the Buddha's hair and nails, to a temple with a stupa in the mountains. Five hundred arhats always stayed there. Morning and evening they burned incense, circled the pagoda, and offered prayers. In those mountains there were five hundred monkeys. They witnessed the men of the Path worshiping at the pagoda, and so they immediately went together to the bank of a deep torrent. Carrying mud and pushing stones they likewise built a stupa. Erecting a tree as a flagstaff, they attached a silk banner at its tip. Morning and evening they worshiped, just as the men of the Path did. The mountain waters then suddenly rose and the five hundred monkeys immediately drowned. Their spirits were reborn in the second or Trāyastriṃśa heaven, in a palace with the seven precious things. Clothing and food came naturally. They all thought: "Where did we come from to be reborn in heaven?" With the heavenly eye each then saw his previous appearance, the body of a monkey. Just like the men of the Path, they were playfully building a pagoda. Although their bodies were drowned, their spirits had attained rebirth in heaven. "We must descend now to show our gratitude to our old corpses!" They all took their servants and with flowers, incense, and music they descended to their old corpses. They scattered the flowers, burned incense, and went seven times around them.

In the mountains at that time there were five hundred brahmans. With their heretical path and heterodox views they did not believe in demerit or merit. When they saw that the heavenly persons were scattering flowers, making music, and walking around the corpses of the monkeys, they asked in amazement: "Gods, your bright reflection is so imposing! Why do you condescend to worship these corpses?" The heavenly persons said: "These corpses are our former bodies. In the past we playfully erected a pagoda here, just as the men of the Path did. When the mountain waters suddenly rose, we drowned. Because of this slight merit we attained rebirth in heaven. That is why we now scatter flowers to show our gratitude to our former bodies. Such is the merit gained by playfully building a pagoda! If you will earnestly serve the Buddha, your merit will be difficult to describe. You gentlemen

590c   hold heterodox views and do not believe in what is right. Toiling for a hundred eons you will not gain a thing. It would be better for you all to go to Mount Gṛdhrakūṭa. The merits gained by serving and offering prayers will be endless." So they all rejoiced and went to where the Buddha was. They prostrated themselves in obeisance, scattered flowers, and offered worship. The heavenly persons said to the Buddha: "Recently we had the bodies of monkeys, but we experienced your kindness, World-honored One, and we attained rebirth in heaven. Regretfully we did not meet you, O Buddha. Therefore we now take refuge!" They again said to the Buddha: "What evil conduct did we do in a previous existence that we experienced those monkey bodies? Even though we built a pagoda, our bodies drowned." The Buddha informed the heavenly persons: "This has a reason. It does not happen out of nowhere. I shall now explain to you how it came about. A long time ago, there were five hundred young brahmans. They all went to the mountains in search of the path of an immortal. In the mountains at that time was an ascetic who wanted to mend his pure abode on the mountain with mud. He went down to get some water. His body was so light, that it seemed like he was flying. The five hundred brahmans were envious and they all laughed at him [saying]: "Now, this ascetic is flying up and down in a hurry, just like a monkey! Why marvel at him! If he does not stop getting water in this way, he will shortly drown once the torrential mountain waters come." The Buddha informed the heavenly persons: "The ascetic who was running up and down at that time was myself. The five hundred brahmans were the five hundred monkeys. They jestingly performed a misdeed and they personally experienced its retribution." Thereupon the World-honored One spoke the stanza:

1. One may jestingly do evil, but having performed the bodily act, one sadly experiences the retribution. Subsequent to the act comes the demerit.

The Buddha informed the heavenly persons: "Even though you were animals in your recent existence, you still could playfully erect a stupa. Now you have attained rebirth in heaven, your sins are extinguished, and you thrive in good fortune. Having returned to earth now, you have personally received the proper teaching. Because of this you will be free from any suffering for a long time." After the Buddha had said this, the five hundred heavenly persons attained the Path. When the five hundred brahmans gathered on the riverbanks heard about the retribution of demerit and merit, they sighed: "We have applied ourselves to [the path of] a seer for quite a number of years, but we have no results yet. The monkeys who playfully perform merit and obtain rebirth in heaven are much better. The qualities of the Buddha's path are so truly wonderful!" Thereupon they kowtowed at the Buddha's feet and wished to become his disciples. When the Buddha said: "Welcome, monks!", they became ascetics. After strenuous daily development they attained the path of the arhat.

Once the Buddha was in a pure abode in the land of Śrāvastī, expounding the Doctrine to gods and men. At that time the second son of the king of the country was called Virūḍhaka. When he was twenty years old his attendants and officials forced out his father the king. He killed his older brother, the crown prince, and made himself king. An evil minister called Na-li said to King 591a Virūḍhaka, "O king, at the time you were crown prince, you went to your [mother's] family home in the land of the Śākyas. When

105

you looked in on the Buddha's pure abode, you were scolded by the sons of the Śākyas, and thoroughly reviled [because of your mother's lowly birth]. At that time, you announced that when you became king, you would see to this. Now the time has come. You should mobilize your troops and horses and exact revenge." He made the necessary arrangements and, leading his soldiers and horses, was about to attack the land of the Śākyas. The Buddha had a second disciple, called Mahāmaudgalyāyana. The disciple saw that King Virūḍhaka was leading his troops to attack the land of the Śākyas and avenge an old grievance, and that he would destroy the four types of disciples. He felt great pity and went to where the Buddha was. He said to the Buddha: "King Virūḍhaka is attacking the land of the Śākyas now. I think that people there will suffer. I want to save the people of the land of the Śākyas with four expedient means: one, I shall move the Śākya people to a place in the sky. Two, I shall move the Śākya people to a place in the ocean. Three, I shall move the Śākya people to a place between two Cakravāda mountains. Four, I shall move the Śākya people to a place in the middle of a big country in another direction. I shall see to it that King Virūḍhaka does not know their whereabouts." The Buddha informed Mahāmaudgalyāyana: "Even though I know that you have the knowledge and virtue that can relocate the people of the land of the Śākyas in a safe place, all things and beings have seven things from which there is no escape. What seven? One, birth. Two, old age. Three, sickness. Four, death. Five, demerit. Six, merit. Seven, causality. Even though one may want to avoid these seven things, one cannot obtain freedom. If you can do this with your supernatural power, the burden of the demerit of the former retribution cannot be left behind." Thereupon Mahāmaudgalyāyana did obeisance and left. According to his own idea he chose four or five thousand friends and *dānapati*s (liberal donors) of the people of the land of the Śākyas, placed them in a vessel, and moved them to the stars in the sky. When King Virūḍhaka had attacked the land of the Śākyas and killed three hundred thousand people, he led his army and returned to his country. Thereupon Mahāmaudgalyāyana went to where the Buddha was. He did obeisance to the Buddha, prided himself, and said: "King Virūḍhaka has attacked the land of the Śākyas. I, your disciple, have saved four or five thousand people of the land of the Śākyas with your supernatural power, O Buddha. They have all escaped into the sky now." The Buddha informed Mahāmaudgalyāyana: "Have you gone and looked at the people in the vessel?" He said: "I have not gone to look at them yet." The Buddha said: "First go and look at the people in the vessel." Mahāmaudgalyāyana let the vessel come down through his power of the Path, and he saw that the people there had all died. Thereupon Mahāmaudgalyāyana was depressed and mournful, and felt sorry for their suffering. He returned and said to the Buddha: "The people in the vessel are all dead now. My virtue and supernatural power were not able to counter the demerit of their former retribution." The Buddha informed Mahāmaudgalyāyana: "There are these seven things. The Buddha and the nobles, the seers and men of the Path may hide them or disperse their bodies, but none can avoid these seven things." Thereupon the World-honored One spoke the stanzas:

2. Neither in the sky, nor in the ocean, nor hiding among the crevices of mountains, is there a place to escape from the misfortune of one's previous evil.

3. All beings suffer and cannot escape from the cycle of old age and death. Only the kind and wise do not have thoughts of others' wrong and evil.

When the Buddha had said this, countless people sitting nearby heard the Buddha's explanation of the doctrine of impermanence. They were all sad, knowing that retribution is hard to avoid. Then they joyfully attained the Path and realized the status of stream-enterer.

591b

Chapter XVIII

The Rod

There once was a country called Hsien-t'i. An aged monk lived there who suffered from a long illness. He was emaciated and filthy. He was lying in a pure abode in Hsien-t'i but no one looked after him. The Buddha led five hundred monks to where he lived. He told the monks to look after him, to make rice gruel for him, but when they smelled his foul place, they despised him. The Buddha had Śakra, ruler of the gods, bring some hot water, and the Buddha himself washed the body of the sick monk with his *vajra* hands. The earth shook and there was a burst of sudden, bright light. Everyone was startled. The king of the land and his subjects, gods, dragons, spirits, and countless people went to where the Buddha was. They kowtowed, did obeisance, and said to the Buddha: "You, O Buddha, are the World-honored One. You are incomparable in the three worlds, possessed of the virtues of the Path. Why do you condescend to wash this sick and filthy monk?" The Buddha informed the king of the land and the whole gathering: "The reason why the Tathāgata has appeared in the world is precisely because of this distressed one, who has no one to look after him. When honoring a sick ascetic, a man of the Path, or any poor and lonely old person, the merit is immeasurable. One's wishes will be fulfilled. Merits will come, just as the five rivers keep flowing. As one's qualities are gradually consummated, one may attain the Path." The king said to the Buddha: "Now what misdeed did this monk previously do, that he is stricken by illness for many years, beyond any cure?" The Buddha informed the king: "There once was a king called O-hsing. His reign was very cruel. He ordered a very strong officer to whip people. Conforming to the king's severity, the officer personally displayed a chilling effect on all. When he wanted to whip someone, he demanded a price. When he obtained something, the whipping was light, but when he obtained nothing, it was heavy. The whole country was sick of him. There was a sage who was accused by someone, and who was to be whipped. He declared to the officer: 'I am a disciple of the Buddha. I never did anything wrong. I am wrongly accused. Please, show some lenience!' When the officer heard that he was a disciple of the Buddha, he used the whip lightly, without touching him. When the officer's life ended, he fell into hell. He was very maliciously flogged, and when his demerit was extinguished, he appeared

591c again, but only to be among animals and be constantly beaten for more than five hundred existences. When his demerit had ended he became a man and was constantly hampered by a grave illness. The pain did not leave him. The king of the land at that time is now Devadatta. The officer is the present sick monk. The sage is myself. In my previous existence I was treated with lenience. The whip did not touch me. That is why I, the World-honored One, personally washed him. When someone performs good or evil, misfortune or good fortune follows him. Even in another birth and death cycle it cannot be avoided." Thereupon the World-honored One spoke the stanzas:

> 1. He who strikes at the virtuous, falsely defaming those who are without offense, his misfortune is tenfold. His calamity is sudden and without pardon.

> 2. He experiences severe pain in his life and his limbs are broken. He ails accordingly. He loses his mind and is confused.

> 3. He stands accused, or he has difficulties with the district magistrate. His riches are completely wasted and he is separated from his relatives.

> 4. His house and possessions go up in flames. When he dies, he goes to hell. Such is the tenfold [misfortune].

Then, when the sick monk had heard these stanzas of the Buddha and the events of his former lives, he acknowledged his former behavior. As he subdued his thoughts and reproved himself, his ailment was instantly cured in front of the Buddha. His person safe and his mind at rest, he attained arhatship. The king of Hsien-t'i was delighted and gained pious understanding. He subsequently received the five precepts and became a pure believer. He carried them out till his death and attained the path of a stream-enterer.

Once the Buddha was in the land of Śrāvastī, in the pure abode of the garden of Anāthapiṇḍada in the Jetavana, expounding the Doctrine to gods, men, dragons, and demons. In the east there was a land called Uttarāvatī. There were five hundred brahmans who were going together to the Ganges River. On its bank there were three sacrificial ponds. By washing away their impurities they sought to become immortals in their nakedness, in accordance with Nirgrantha (Jain) law. Their way led through a vast marsh, and they got lost and could not pass it. They had become short on provisions along the way, and looking from a distance they saw movement in a tree which appeared as if alive with a spirit. They thought someone was there and rushed to the tree. When they realized there was nothing, the brahmans raised their voices and lamented loudly. They were distressed by hunger and thirst and dying of exhaustion in this marsh. The spirit of the tree appeared as a man and asked the brahmans: "Men of the Path, where do you come from and where do you want to go now?" They replied with one voice: "We want to go to the divine ponds and cleanse ourselves, hoping to become immortals. Today we are hungry and thirsty. Have pity, we pray, and mercifully come to our aid!" The spirit of the tree then raised his hands, and food and drink of a hundred flavors abundantly flowed from his hands, giving them all the food and drink required. When they were all fully fed and satisfied, the remaining food and drink were adequate to keep them supplied for the rest of the way. When they were about to part, they went to the spirit and asked: "What virtuous deed did you previously perform that you bring about such loftiness?" The spirit answered the brahmans: "I formerly lived in the land of Śrāvastī. The high official of the land was then called Sudatta. Providing food for the Buddha and his monks, he bought koumiss on the market, but there was no one to pick it up. He looked all over and finally engaged me to pick it up. We went to the pure abode and he let me pour it. After they had passed around the water to cleanse themselves, I solemnly listened to the Doctrine. We were all glad, judging it to be immeasurably wholesome. I then fasted and did not eat upon my return in the evening. My wife asked in surprise: 'I wonder what is bothering you!' I answered: 'Nothing. When I was walking in the market, I saw the elder Sudatta and we both gave food to the Buddha in the park. He invited me to fast, the fast being one of the eight prohibitions.' My wife became angry and said with indignation: 'Gautama confuses the common [people]. How could one take up with him! If you do not forget about him, trouble will come from it!' As she kept pressuring me, I ate with her. Then, at night, my life's fortunes ended at midnight. As a spirit I came to be born here. Because my foolish wife ruined my rules of fasting and because I did not complete those deeds, I came to be born in this marsh and became the spirit of this tree. As for the merit of picking up the koumiss, from my hands come food and drink. If I had completed the rules of fasting, I would have been reborn in heaven. The results are experienced accordingly." He then pronounced the stanza to the brahmans:

> 5. Sacrifices sow the roots of calamity, just as night and day, creepers grow. Severe suffering ruins the body, but with the rules of fasting, one transcends the world to become an immortal.

When the brahmans had heard the stanza, their confusion was cleared. They piously accepted it and turned around back to Śrāvastī. Their way led through a country named Kauśāmbī. There was an elder, called Ghoṣila, who was kind to others and respected by all. When the brahmans passed by his lodging, the elder asked: "Men of the Path, where do you come from, and where do want to go now?" They reported everything about the marsh and the excellence of the spirit of the tree. "We want to go to Śrāvastī and to where Sudatta is. Choosing the rules of fasting, we long to receive them and obtain merit." Ghoṣila was in raptures of joy. Influenced by his former conduct, he had a continual understanding. He proclaimed that those of his kindred who could go with him and receive the regulations of fasting should unite with the five hundred men and answer his call. He vowed to lead them. They all talked it over and left with dignity. They all went to Śrāvastī. Before he had reached the Jetavana, he encountered Sudatta on this way. He looked back and asked his followers who this man was. They answered: "Sudatta." The crowd of brahmans was glad. They followed, saying: "Our wish is fulfilled! We were looking for him, and we found him." They rushed to meet him and unanimously said in praise: "The spirit of the tree has praised your virtue. Respectfully and candidly he has fully explained his admiration. That is why we have come to place ourselves in your care. We hope that you will instruct us in fasting according to the Doctrine!" He stopped his carriage and answered: "Your quest is very wholesome. I have a revered teacher, called the Tathāgata. He helps mankind. These days he lives in the Jetavana. We may all go to him in friendship." They respectfully assented and reverentially went forward. When they met with the Tathāgata, their gladness was hard to measure. They fell prostrate in obeisance, withdrew, and sat aside. They all knelt deeply and said to the World-honored One: "We initially left home and wanted to go to the three ponds to cleanse ourselves and seek to be immortals. 592b Passing by the spirit of a tree, he gave us the explanation. That is why we submit ourselves to be converted. Please, show us your supreme spirituality!" Thereupon, because of their behavior, the World-honored One expounded the stanzas:

> 6. One may be naked and cut one's hair, submit to the rod
> and wear a coarse garment; one may cleanse oneself
> squatting on a rock; but how could his doubts be undone?

7. When he does not attack, kill, or burn, and when he does not seek to win but is kind and loving toward the world, there is no enmity where he goes.

When the five hundred brahmans had heard the stanzas, they were very glad. They all became ascetics and attained the path of arhatship. Ghoṣila and his kindred obtained the eye of the Doctrine. The monks said to the Buddha: "What virtuous deed had the five hundred brahmans and elders previously done to obtain the Path so swiftly?" The World-honored One informed them: "A long, long time ago, there was a Buddha in the world called Kāśyapa. He explained to his disciples that I would come at the time of the five defilements. At that time there were a thousand brahmans and elders who said these same words: 'Let us meet the Buddha Śākyamuni!' The brahmans of that time are now these brahmans. The elders of that time are now those with Ghoṣila. That is why they have met me and have understood." The monks were very glad, did obeisance, and followed the instructions.

Volume Three

Chapter XIX

Similes with Old Age

Once the Buddha was in the land of Śrāvastī in the pure abode of the Jetavana. After his meal he expounded the Doctrine of immortality to gods and men, to the ruler, to his ministers and his people, and to the four classes of disciples. Then there were seven elder brahmans from afar who had come to where the Buddha was. They kowtowed, folded their hands together, and said to the Buddha: "We strangers would humbly like to listen to your noble way of conversion. We should have taken refuge a long time ago, but there were many impediments. Now that we have arrived and observed your noble complexion, we wish to be your disciples and extinguish all suffering." When the Buddha had accepted them as ascetics, he told the seven men to stay together in one quarter. But after these seven men had seen the World-honored One, and subsequently were able to practice his Path, they did not reflect on the nature of impermanence. They sat together in their quarters, just thinking of worldly things. They were speaking in a low tone or loudly laughing, not reflecting on success or failure. Their lives were daily nearing the end, time was running out. They were just laughing with joy together, confused about the three realms 592c of existence. With his three penetrating knowledges, the Buddha knew that their lives were about to end. He felt sorry for them. He stood up, went to their quarters, and informed them: "Sirs, when

115

you practice the Path, you must seek to surpass worldly things. Why do you laugh so loudly? All beings rely on five things. What are the five? One, they rely on their youth. Two, they rely on their upright appearance. Three, they rely on their great strength. Four, they rely on their wealth. Five, they rely on their noble family. While you, seven sirs, are speaking in a low tone or loudly laughing, what do you rely on?" Thereupon the World-honored One spoke the stanzas:

> 1. Why joy and why laughter, when mindfulness should always be ablaze! Profoundly shrouded in darkness, it would be better to seek for light.

> 2. Looking at oneself, appearance is one's model. Relying on it is considered to be safe, but it is the source of a great deal of imagining that brings forth illness. How could one know it is not real!

> 3. When one becomes old, beauty fades. When ill, one loses luster. The skin slackens and muscles shrink. The fate of death is close.

> 4. When the body dies, the spirit goes, just like a driver abandoning his chariot. When the flesh has dissipated and the bones are scattered, how can one rely on a body!

After the Buddha had spoken the stanzas, the seven monks understood. Their [false] expectations ceased and they attained arhatship in front of the Buddha.

Once the Buddha was in a pure abode in Śravasti, expounding the Doctrine to gods and men and to the ruler. Then there was a village of brahmans. In the more than five hundred houses there were five hundred young brahmans, practicing their brahmanical arts. They were arrogant and did not respect their elders. They considered haughtiness and self-importance normal. The five hundred brahmans discussed among themselves: "The ascetic Gautama calls himself a Buddha, with the expedient knowledge of the three penetrating insights. There is none who dares argue with him. Let us invite him for a discussion. Let us question him on different points and we shall know how he is." They then prepared offerings and invited the Buddha. The Buddha went with his disciples to the village of the brahmans. They took their seats, passed the water around, and, after the meal, they washed their hands. Then there were two elder brahmans, man and wife. They happened to be on their begging round in the village. The Buddha knew that formerly they had been very wealthy beyond compare, and that they had been high officials. So the Buddha asked the young brahmans: "Do you know the elder brahmans?" They all said yes. He further asked: "What were they like before?" They said: "They were high officials before, with countless riches." "Then 593a why are they now on their begging round?" They all said: "Their wastefulness was unprincipled. That is why they remain poor." The Buddha said to the brahmans: "In the world there are four things which men [usually] are unable to practice. But he who does them obtains prosperity and does not become poor. What are the four? One, when in the prime of life and strong, do not be arrogant! Two, keep zeal at an advanced age and have no desire for debauchery! Three, when you possess riches and precious things, be constantly mindful of giving! Four, take up studies with a teacher and accept his true words! This elder brahman did not do these four things. He thought his condition was permanent, and he did not reflect on success or failure. Suddenly came disintegration. He is like an old heron waiting by the empty pond, never catching anything." Thereupon the World-honored One spoke the stanzas:

> 5. If one is indolent night and day and does not stop debauchery when old, if one possesses riches but does not practice giving, and if one does not accept the Buddha's words, one will be oppressed by these four [things] and defraud himself.

> 6. Alas, old age is here! Beauty changes to old age. When one is young everything goes as one pleases, but when old, one is trampled down.

7. If one has not practiced pure conduct and has not acquired wealth, in old age one is like a heron, watching an empty pond.

8. If one does not keep the precepts and has not accumulated wealth, in old age one will be emaciated and his energy exhausted. What is there to gain by reflecting on the past!

9. In old age one is like an autumn leaf and walks in a shabby garment. As life goes by swiftly and abandonment is constantly present, regrets are useless.

The Buddha informed the brahmans: "In a generation there are four periods during which one may gain merit by practicing the Path. In this way, one may obtain salvation and escape from any suffering. What are the four? One, the period in which one possesses strength in youth. Two, the period in which one possesses property when rich and honored. Three, the period in which one has experienced the fine field of merit of the Buddha, Dharma, and Sangha. Four, the period in which, when reflecting on things, one feels the sorrow of parting. When one experiences these four things, one's wishes will all be fulfilled. One will certainly gain the Path." Thereupon the World-honored One spoke the stanzas:

10. Night and day life will come to an end, but one may exert oneself at the right opportunity. The world is truly impermanent. Do not doubt that you will fall into the underworld.

11. Apply yourself to kindling the lamp of your mind! Train yourself and seek wisdom! Be free from impurity and do not be tainted! Hold up a candle and contemplate the place of the Path!

When the Buddha said this, he emitted a bright light, illuminating heaven and earth. The five hundred young brahmans then understood. They straightened their clothes and hair, stood up, and did obeisance at the Buddha's feet. They said to the Buddha: "We take refuge in you, World-honored One! We wish to be your disciples." The Buddha said: "Welcome, monks!", and they immediately became ascetics and attained arhatship. The villagers, young and old, all attained the Path, and there was none who was not glad.

Chapter XX

Holding Oneself Dear

Once there was a land called Tāmra. Seven *li* from the city there was a pure abode. Five hundred ascetics constantly dwelled there reading the scriptures and practicing the Path. There was an old monk called Mahallaka. As a person he was not bright. The five hundred men of the Path had to instruct him, but he did not master a single stanza in the course of several years. The whole community despised him and the people did not share their gatherings with him. He always stayed in the pure abode and was ordered to clean up the premises. Later, when the king of the land invited the men of the Path to come to his palace to conduct worship, the monk Mahallaka said to himself: "I was born into this world so dull that I do not know one stanza and I am held in contempt by the others. What a life this is!" So he took a rope and went underneath a big tree in the garden in the rear, intent on hanging himself. With his eye of the Path the Buddha saw this from afar. He transformed himself into the spirit of the tree. He appeared half as a human being and reprimanded him, saying: "Oh monk! Why do you do this?" Mahallaka then fully informed him of his hardship. The transformed spirit reprimanded him, saying: "You cannot do this! Yes, listen to my words! Once, at the time of the Buddha Kāśyapa, you were a Tripiṭaka (learned) ascetic with five hundred disciples. Because of your great learning you despised all others. Sparing of the meaning of the scriptures, you initially would not teach anything. Therefore in every existence you were born into, your faculties were dull. You have only yourself to blame! Why destroy yourself?" Thereupon

121

the World-honored One showed his divinely brilliant appearance and spoke the stanzas:

1. If someone holds himself dear, he should cautiously watch over what should be guarded. If in his aspirations he wants to understand, he should apply himself to what is right without resting.

2. Oneself being first, one should study by oneself. Having profited, one may instruct others. If one is not remiss, one is a sage.

3. When applying oneself one should first correct oneself and correct others later. A well-regulated person acquires wisdom. He certainly changes into a superior person.

4. If one cannot benefit oneself, how can one benefit others? When the mind is regulated and the body correct, what wish will not be fulfilled?

5. What one has initiated earlier, one will later experience. The evildoer experiences evil himself, just as surely as a diamond pierces a pearl.

When the monk Mahallaka had witnessed the Buddha's brilliant personal appearance, he trembled with both grief and joy and kowtowed at the Buddha's feet. He reflected on the meaning of the stanzas and immediately entered the state of concentrative mind. In the presence of the Buddha he subsequently attained arhatship. He knew countless matters of his former lives, and penetrated the essence of all the scriptures of the Tripiṭaka. The Buddha told Mahallaka to don his robe, take his bowl, and have a meal in the king's palace, where he was to preside over five hundred men of the Path. "These men of the Path were your five hundred disciples in your previous existence. If you again expound the Doctrine to them, you will help them obtain the Path and make the king understand and believe in the nature of evil and merit." He at once accepted the Buddha's instructions.

He went straight to the palace and sat down on the seat of 593c
honor. The assembled monks all became angry and wondered why,
but they respected the king's intention and did not dare scold him.
They thought Mahallaka was foolish and did not have any understanding about donations (*dakṣiṇā*) and that thinking was too
exhausting for him. The king then put down his food and he personally poured for him. Mahallaka then gave him a donation [of
the Doctrine]. He sounded like the tremor of thunder, and his clear
words came down like rain. The men of the Path who were sitting
were startled. They repented and all attained arhatship. Expounding the Doctrine to the king, there was nothing he did not explain.
All ministers and officials attained the path of the stream-enterer.

Once the Buddha was in the land of Śrāvastī. There were five hundred brahmans who were constantly seeking advantage over the
Buddha. They wanted to defame him, but the Buddha knew their
thoughts by means of his three penetrating insights. He felt pity
for them and wanted to save them, but their condition had not
matured yet, and the causal condition was not yet at hand. When
all their demerits and merits were in the proper condition, he naturally would bring on the causal condition to match up with their
demerit and merit. These brahmans had previously had some
merit, and they deserved to be saved; their merit had led them on
and brought about an appropriate way.

The five hundred brahmans deliberated among themselves and
said: "We shall make a butcher kill some living creatures and invite the Buddha and his community of monks. The Buddha will
most certainly accept the invitation and praise the butcher, at
which point we shall come forward and deride him." Thereupon
the butcher invited the Buddha for them. The Buddha immediately accepted the invitation, and informed the butcher: "When a
fruit is ripe it falls, and when merit has matured one is saved."
While the butcher went back to provide for food, the Buddha led
his disciples to the village of the butcher, to the house of the
dānapati (liberal donor). The brahmans, young and old, were all

glad. "Today we shall take advantage of the Buddha! If he praises the merit of the *dānapati,* we shall use this to deride him, because, before and after, he has killed living beings and performed demerit. If the Buddha explains the original demerit, we shall rebuke him for today's merit. In either case we shall now have the advantage over the Buddha!" When the Buddha arrived, he sat down, [and the butcher] passed around the water and put down the food. Thereupon the World-honored One contemplated the thoughts of the crowd. They deserved to be saved. So he stuck out his tongue, covering his face and licking his ears. He put forth a bright light, illuminating the whole city. With his divine voice he expounded the stanzas, incanting:

> 6. When a sage teaches, he moves people with the Path. An ignorant one hates this, and he commits evil when he sees it. By committing evil he becomes evil, just as sowing the seeds of bitterness [enhances bitterness].

> 7. Evil collects its own demerit, and good collects its own merit. They all have their own maturation, and they do not mutually cross each other. By practicing what is good, one obtains good, just as sowing something sweet [produces something sweet].

After the Buddha had spoken the stanzas, the minds of the five hundred brahmans opened up in understanding. They immediately came forward and did obeisance to the Buddha. They fell prostrate, folded their hands together, and said to the Buddha: "We were foolish and degraded. We did not thoroughly understand your noble teaching. We only hope for your kind instruction in order to become ascetics!" The Buddha accepted them and they all became ascetics. When the villagers, young and old, had seen the Buddha's transformation, there was none who was not delighted. They all attained the Path and were called noble ones, without any further reference to a butcher. When the meal was over, the Buddha returned to his pure abode.

594a

124

Chapter XXI

The World

Once there was a brahman king called To-wei-hsieh. The king practiced ninety-six kinds of heresies. One day he suddenly had a wholesome thought that he wanted to practice extensive giving. As was the rule for brahmans, he accumulated the seven precious things mountain-high and used them for his giving. When someone came begging, he would allow him to take one handful and leave. This went on for several days, but the hoard did not decrease. The Buddha knew that this king deserved salvation for his previous merit. He changed into a brahman and went to his land. The king came out to meet him. They exchanged greetings, and he asked him how he was and said: "What do you seek? There shouldn't be any difficulty!" The brahman answered: "I come from afar. I would like to beg for some precious jewels and use them to build my dwelling." The king said: "Very well! Take a handful and go!" The brahman took a handful, went seven steps, returned and put the handful back in its original place. The king asked: "Why do you not take them?" The brahman replied: "This is just enough to build a house. Afterwards I shall take a wife. Then it will not suffice for both instances. That is why I do not take anything." The king said: "Take three handfuls!" So the brahman took them, went seven steps, returned again, and put them back in their original place. When the king asked the brahman why he had acted in this way again, he replied: "This will do to take a wife. But then, I will not have any left for the fields, servants, oxen, or horses. I calculate that again it will not suffice. That is why I ceased to act." When the king told him to take seven handfuls, the brahman took them, went seven steps, returned again and put them back. The king said: "What is on your mind now?" The brahman answered: "When I have sons and daughters, they will marry too. For their expenses in good or bad fortune, I calculate that this will not do. That is why I do not take anything." The king said: "Take the whole hoard of precious things! I give it to you!" The brahman accepted, but then cast them aside. The king was utterly surprised and again asked why. The brahman answered: "I was actually begging in order to provide myself with a livelihood. But when one truly thinks about life, one does not remain long in the world. Everything is impermanent, and day and night it is difficult to remain stable. Causality proceeds, one thing after another, and suffering deepens daily. Accumulating precious things mountain-high does not benefit oneself. While covetousness is scheming, one inopportunely brings suffering to oneself. It would be better to appease one's mind and seek for the unconditioned Path. That is why I do not take anything." The king's mind opened up, and he wished to serve the illuminating teaching. Thereupon the brahman manifested the splendid luminous appearance of the Buddha. He leaped in the air and spoke the stanzas:

> 1. Even if one had a hoard of precious jewels as high as heaven or even if they were to fill the world, it would still be better to experience the Path.

> 594b
> 2. What is unwholesome appears to be wholesome, and what is lovely appears to be unlovely. What is painful appears to be pleasant, but the madman is destroyed by this.

Then, when the king saw that the Buddha's splendid appearance illuminated heaven and earth, and when he further heard these stanzas, he was in raptures of delight and joy. The king and his ministers then accepted the five precepts and they attained the path of stream-enterer.

Chapter XXII

Speaking about the Buddha

Once the Buddha was in the region of Magadha, underneath the tree of great joy (Bodhi Tree), the most excellent spot of the Path. Having subdued Māra by the strength of his virtue, he was sitting and reflecting: "May the drum of the law of immortality be heard in the trichiliocosmos. Formerly, the king, my father, sent five men. When I was sent offerings of rice gruel, they maintained their austerity. The reward for their merit should be conferred!" These five men were in the land of Benares. When the Tathāgata stood up under the tree, his majestic demeanor with the primary and secondary marks radiated across heaven and earth, and his imposing spirit caused [the earth] to tremble, bringing joy to those who saw it. He went to the land of Benares, but prior to his arrival he met on his way a brahman called Upaka. He had parted with his relatives and left his house in search of a teacher, applying himself to the Path. Looking up to His Revered Excellence, he felt a mingling of fright and joy. He descended by the side of the road, raised his voice and said in praise: "Your imposing spirit moves people and your dignified demeanor is outstanding. What teacher have you served, that you have obtained this countenance?" The Buddha spoke the following stanzas to Upaka:

> 1. The eightfold right [path] was a self-awakening by myself! I cannot leave it and I am untainted. My craving has ceased, and I have destroyed the web of desire. I am thus by myself, without receiving instruction from a teacher.

2. I do not have a teacher or witness for my conduct. In my resolve I am alone, without companion. Having completed everything, I have become a Buddha, and thus have I understood the Noble Path.

Upon hearing the stanzas Upaka was downhearted, for he did not understand. So he asked the World-honored One: "Gautama, where are you going?" The Buddha informed the brahman: "I want to go to the land of Benares, to beat the drum of the Doctrine of immortality and to turn its unsurpassed wheel. Among the multitude of sages of the three worlds there has never been anyone who, as I will do now, has turned the wheel of the Doctrine, to lead the people to enter nirvana." Upaka was overjoyed. "Excellent, excellent it is when you say so, O Buddha! Please open up immortality in accordance with the Doctrine which ought to be expounded!" After saluting the Buddha, he went on his way. As he had not yet reached his teacher, he spent the night along the way. Late at night his life suddenly ended. When the Buddha saw with his eye of the Path that he had died, he felt pity for him and said: "The world of beings is foolish in thinking that life has permanence. Having met the Buddha and departed, he has perished alone. When the drum of the Doctrine reverberates, he alone will not hear it. When immortality extinguishes suffering, he alone will not taste it. He will keep turning in the five predestinations and his birth and death cycle will go on. Passing through a number of eons, when will he be saved?" The Buddha in his compassion spoke the stanzas:

3. Having seen the truth, pure and without defilement, and having crossed the abyss of the five predestinations, a Buddha has arisen, illuminating the world in order to do away with all suffering.

594c

4. It is difficult to be born in the human destination as well as to obtain one's full span of life. It is difficult [i.e., rare] for the world to have a Buddha, and it is not easy to hear and grasp the Buddha's Doctrine.

When the Buddha had spoken these stanzas, five hundred gods and men in the sky heard them. They were delighted and all attained the path of the stream-enterer.

[The section (T.601b16–601c22) has been moved to this location (between T.594c5 and T.594c6).]

Four thousand *li* south of Rājagṛha there once was a land which served several thousands of brahmans. In the land there was a great drought then, without rain for three years. They prayed to the gods everywhere. The king asked the brahmans the reason for this, and they said: "We shall practice abstinence. After that we shall send someone to the god Brahmā to inquire about this disaster." The king said: "Very well! Please inform me about what you need for the abstinence [ceremony]." The brahmans said: "We shall need twenty chariots with firewood, ghee, honey, oil, flower-incense, a baldachin and streamers, and sacrificial vessels of gold and silver. We need all that." So the king took care of their requirements. They left the city and on a level ground seven *li* from the city they piled up the firewood as high as a mountain. They exhorted one another: "Those who are not sparing of their life will finally be reborn in the brahma heaven. Let us choose seven men. They must go into the fire and we shall send them to the brahma heaven." After the seven men had been selected and received the sacrificial incantations, they were coerced into mounting the pyre. They lit the fire from below to burn them to death. The smoke and flames were scorching and when the heat came straight at them, the seven men were alarmed. They asked for help left and right, but there was no one who could help. They raised their voices and said: "If only there were someone in the three realms who had great pity and thought of our distress! Please, let us take refuge!" The Buddha knew this from afar, and hearing their voices he went to their rescue. He manifested his primary and secondary auspicious marks in the sky. When the seven men saw the Buddha, they jumped with both grief and joy. "We wish

601c

129

to take refuge! Save us from this painful heat!" Thereupon the World-honored One spoke the stanzas:

> 5. Some often take refuge in the spirits of mountains, rivers, and trees. They place pictures and pray to them to seek blessings.

> 6. Such refuges are not auspicious nor the best. They cannot come and save you from any suffering.

> 7. When one takes refuge in the Buddha, his Doctrine, and the congregation of monks, and in the four noble truths and the qualities of the Path, one is certain to be seen in right wisdom.

> 8. The cycle of birth and death is extreme suffering, but one can be saved from it by the [four noble] truths. They save one from the eight hardships in the world as well as prevent the rise of suffering.

> 9. Taking refuge in the Buddha, Dharma, and Sangha is the most auspicious and the best. Yes, only such a one is saved from all suffering.

After the Buddha had spoken the stanzas, the crackling of the fire was consequently silenced. The seven men were safe and immeasurably happy. The brahmans and the people in the land were all startled, and they looked up with respect. The bright appearance of the World-honored One was glorious. He divided himself and scattered his limbs. Disappearing in the east, he appeared in the west, appearing and disappearing at will. He emitted water and fire from his person, and the five colors were dazzling. When the multitude saw this, they fully took refuge. Thereupon the seven men descended from the pyre. With grief and joy intermingled they spoke the stanzas:

> 10. To meet a sage is happiness, and to be close to him is also happiness. Being far from any foolish person, one is happy all alone, doing what is wholesome.

11. Preserving one's proper insight is happiness, and furthermore expounding the Doctrine is happiness. Absence of strife in the world and embodiment of the precepts provide constant happiness.

12. To let a sage stay is happiness, associating intimately with him as a relative. Being near to a wise person, one's learning becomes lofty and far-reaching.

Thereupon, after the seven men had spoken these stanzas, all the brahmans wished to be disciples too. The Buddha immediately accepted them. They all became ascetics and attained arhatship. The king and his subjects all cultivated the Path. It subsequently rained heavily and as the land prospered, the people were happy. Conversions to the Path increased, and there was none who did not aspire to learning.

Chapter XXIII

Happiness

Once, three hundred *li* southeast of Rājagṛha, there was a village of mountain people with over five hundred homes. They were un-yielding as people and difficult to convert to the Path. Through their merits in a former world they deserved to be saved, and there-upon the World-honored One transformed himself into an ascetic. He went to the village to beg for alms. After he had begged for alms, he left the village and sat down under a tree and entered *samādhi* (concentration) on nirvana. For seven days he did not pant, breathe, move, or turn. When the villagers saw this, they thought his life had ended. They said to one another: "The ascetic is dead. We shall all give him a burial." Each took a bundle of firewood for the pyre. When the fire was lit and the firewood used up, the Buddha rose from his seat and manifested his divine transformation of the Path. His light was brilliantly shining and moving in the ten directions. After he had manifested the transformation, he returned to his seat underneath the tree. His bearing was peaceful and delightful, just as before. The villagers, young and old, were all startled. They kowtowed and apologized: "Mountain people are insensitive. They do not recognize a super-natural person. We were wrong to burn you with firewood, but you are the same as before the burning. We consider the misdeed we have done to be greater than Mount T'ai. Do deign mercifully to pardon us! Do not censure us with enmity! We were ignorant of why you, O supernatural person, are free from any illness or grief, or why you are not hungry or thirsty, or why you did not suffer from heat!" Thereupon the World-honored One smiled with a peaceful complexion and spoke the stanzas:

1. My life is at peace. I do not feel hurt by enmity. While everyone has enmity, I conduct myself without enmity.

2. My life is at peace. I am not ill with any illness. While everyone has illness, I conduct myself without illness.

3. My life is at peace. I do not grieve by sorrow. While everyone has sorrow, I conduct myself without sorrow.

4. My life is at peace. I am pure and unconditioned. Happiness is my food, just as for the Shining Gods.

595a 5. My life is at peace, calm and unconcerned. How could the fire from a countrywide heap of firewood burn me?

Then, when the five hundred men in the village had heard him expound the stanzas, they all became ascetics and attained arhatship. All the villagers, young and old, believed in the Buddha, Dharma, and Sangha. The Buddha quickly went to the Bamboo Grove together with the five hundred men. When the sage Ānanda had seen that the Buddha had come together with those who had attained the Path, he came forward and said to the Buddha: "What special qualities do these monks have that they make you, World-honored One, personally go to save them?" The Buddha informed the Reverend Ānanda: "When I had not yet become a Buddha, there was in the world a *pratyekabuddha* (aspirant to Buddhahood) who usually stayed in these mountains. Under a tree not far from a village he wanted to enter *parinirvāṇa* (nirvana after death). He showed his supernatural qualities of the Path and immediately attained nirvana. The villagers took firewood and set fire to the pyre. They gathered his relics, put them in a precious urn, and buried it on a mountain top. They all had an earnest wish, which was to obtain the Path later. The nirvana of such an ascetic was a joyous event! Because of this merit they deserved to obtain the Path. That is why I, the Tathāgata, went to save them!" When the Buddha had said this, countless gods and men all attained the Path.

Once the Buddha was in a pure abode in Śrāvastī. There were four monks who were sitting under a tree. They asked one another:

"What is most sorrowful in the whole world?" One said: "Among the sorrows in the world none surpasses lust." One said: "Among the sorrows in the world none surpasses anger." One said: "Among the sorrows in the world none surpasses hunger and thirst." Another said: "Among the sorrows in the world none surpasses fear." Their dispute about the meaning of sorrow went on without end. The Buddha knew what they were disputing and went to where they were. He asked the monks: "What are you arguing about?" They then stood up, did obeisance, and gave a full explanation of what they were arguing about. The Buddha said to the monks: "Your arguments do not measure up to the meaning of sorrow. Among the sorrows in the world none surpasses the possession of a body. Hunger and thirst, cold and heat, anger, fear, lust, and misfortune or enmity, all come from the body. The body is the source of all sorrows and the origin of calamities. It makes one's thoughts weary and brings extreme anxiety. Its stress is ten-thousandfold. Wriggling in the three realms, one is malicious to another. When one is attached to a self, the birth and death cycle does not cease. It all comes from the body. If one wants to leave worldly suffering, one must seek for quietude. If one properly guards the body and controls his thoughts, and is tranquil and without the rise of any vain imaginings, one may obtain nirvana. This is the utmost pleasure." Thereupon the World-honored One spoke these stanzas:

6. No heat surpasses lust and no poison surpasses anger.
No suffering surpasses the body and no ordinary pleasure
surpasses nirvana.

7. What is without pleasure is of little joy, small disputation, and minimal wisdom. If one seeks what is great
through contemplation, one obtains the great pleasure.

8. I am the World-honored One. I have long understood
what it is to be free from grief. I have rightly transcended
the three realms and I alone have subdued the Māras.

595b After the Buddha had spoken the stanzas, he informed the monks: "Formerly, countless ages ago, there was a monk with the five superknowledges called Atibalavīryaparākrama. In solitude underneath a tree in the mountains he sought the Path. Then there were also four creatures who always maintained their security in his neighborhood. The first was a pigeon, the second a crow, the third a venomous snake, and the fourth a deer. These four creatures went looking for food in the daytime, and in the evening they returned to spend the night. One night the four creatures asked each other: 'What is the most serious cause of sorrow in the world?' The crow said: 'Hunger and thirst are the most serious. When I am hungry and thirsty my body becomes lean, my vision is blurred, and my spirit is uneasy. I may throw myself into a net and have no regard for weapons. While we are destroyed, there is nothing that does not come from them. Speaking in this way, hunger and thirst do cause sorrow.' The pigeon said: 'Lust is the most serious cause of sorrow. When lust is ablaze, I am not mindful of anything. It endangers the body and destroys life. There is nothing that does not come from it.' The venomous snake said: 'Anger is the most serious cause of sorrow. As soon as a poisonous thought has arisen, it does not even distinguish near or distant relatives. Yes, it can kill someone, or it can turn on oneself.' The deer said: 'Fear is the most serious cause of sorrow. When I am in the wilds, I am always frightened at heart. I am afraid of hunters and wolves. When I hear but their faintest sound, I flee to the edge [of the forest]. Mother and child abandon each other. I shiver deep inside of me. Speaking in this way, fear is the cause of sorrow.' When the monk had heard this, he told them: 'What you are arguing about is the end result; you do not examine the root of sorrow. Among the sorrows in the world none surpasses the possession of a body. The body is the receptacle for suffering. Its apprehensions are immeasurable. That is why I have left the worldly realm to apply myself to the Path. I extinguish my bad thoughts and do away with imaginings. I do not covet the four great elements. I want to cut off the origin of suffering, intent on achieving nirvana. The path of nirvana is quietude and formlessness. When one's distress has forever ended, he will know great peace.' When the four creatures heard this, their minds opened up." The Buddha informed the monks: "The monk with the five superknowledges at that time was myself. The four creatures then are you four people now. In a previous existence, you had already heard the meaning of the root of suffering; why then did you argue again?" When the monks heard this, they felt ashamed and reproved themselves. Immediately they attained arhatship in the presence of the Buddha.

Chapter XXIV

Pleasure

Once, when the Buddha was in a pure abode in Śrāvastī, there were four monks in their first stages of study. They went underneath a mango tree to sit in meditative practice of the Path. The mango blossoms were in full bloom with fine colors and pleasant fragrance. So they said to each other: "Among the ten thousand things in the world, which one is most lovable and lifts up one's feelings?" One monk said: "Roaming around in the plains in the second month of spring when the hundred trees are in full boom, this is utmost pleasure." Another said: "Drinking wine together during a happy occasion with relatives, and playing music, song, and dance, these are utmost pleasures." Another said: "Accumulating riches and gratifying one's desires. Having one's carriages, horses, and personal adornments different from those of the rest 595c of the crowd. When one's splendor is manifest, coming and going, and when people keep gazing, this is utmost pleasure." Another monk said: "When one's wives are just right, their ornamented garments fresh and new, when their perfume is fragrant, and when they give rein to the passions as one likes, this is utmost pleasure." The Buddha knew that the four persons deserved to be saved, but that they had thoughts about the six desires without considering their own impermanence. So he called the four monks and asked them: "While you were sitting there together under a tree, what were you discussing?" When the four monks truthfully related what they were most happy about, the Buddha informed the four: "What you were discussing is completely in the path of distress and great danger. It is not the way of enduring peace and utmost pleasure. All things flourish in spring but decay in autumn and winter. One's relatives may mean joy and pleasure, but they will all go away. Riches, carriages, and horses become the shares of the five families. The beauty of wives rules love and hate. When a common man dwells in the worldly realm, he gives rise to the misfortune of enmity. He endangers himself and exterminates his own family. His sorrows are immeasurable. The suffering of the three woeful destinations and the eight hardships are enormous. There is nothing that does not come from them! Therefore, monks, reject the worldly realm and seek for the Path! Set your mind on the unconditioned and do not covet splendor! Attaining nirvana is utmost pleasure." Thereupon the World-honored One spoke the stanzas:

1. What is loved brings distress and what is loved also brings fear. Without love (for things), wherewith the distress and wherewith the fear?

2. Affection brings distress and affection also brings fear. Without any affection, wherewith the distress and wherewith the fear?

3. Covetousness brings distress and covetousness also brings fear. If one is freed from any covetousness, wherewith the distress and wherewith the fear?

4. When one longs for the Doctrine and moral conduct is fulfilled, when one is utterly sincere and knows shame, and when one approaches the Path in one's personal conduct, one is held dear by the crowd.

5. When it is possible that desire does not arise, when one thinks what is right and tells it so, and when one's mind is free from covetousness, one is certain to cross the stream and be delivered.

The Buddha informed the four monks: "Once there was a king called P'u-an. He was on friendly terms with the four kings of his neighboring countries. He invited these four kings to a feast, and for a whole month they wined and dined and amused themselves. They were merry beyond compare. On the day of parting King P'u-an asked the four kings: 'Living in the world, what do you think is most pleasant?' One king said: 'Games are most pleasant.' Another king said: 'A happy meeting with relatives and music are most pleasant.' Another king said: 'When, while amassing many riches, one's desires are in accord with one's wishes, this is most pleasant.' Another king said: 'Giving reign to one's passions in lust, this is most pleasant.' King P'u-an said: 'What you are discussing, sirs, is the basis of suffering, the origin of distress. First comes happiness, but later comes suffering and the sorrows are ten-thousandfold. They are all caused by them. It would be better to be at rest, without any longing or desires, and to be dispassionate and keep one's concentration. Obtaining the Path issues forth happiness.' When the four kings heard this, they were delighted and gained pious understanding." The Buddha informed the monks: "King P'u-an at the time was myself. The four kings were the four of you. We had this discussion before. Therefore I shall not offer any explanation now. The birth and death cycle goes on as creepers grow. How can one rest at all?" Then, when the four monks had heard these meaningful words again, they felt shame and remorse for their error. But their minds opened up. They extinguished their evil thoughts, eradicated their desires, and attained arhatship.

596a

Chapter XXV

Anger

Once the Buddha was on Mount Gṛdhrakūṭa in Rājagṛha. Devadatta and King Ajātaśatru were discussing how to destroy the Buddha and his disciples. The king ordered his countrymen not to serve the Buddha. When the Buddha's community of monks went begging for alms, they could not receive any donation. The Venerable Śāriputra, Maudgalyāyana, Kāśyapa, and Subhūti, and also the nuns, such as Mahāprajāpatī, all led their disciples to another country. Only the Buddha and five hundred arhats stayed on Mount Gṛdhrakūṭa. Devadatta went to King Ajātaśatru and consulted with the king: "The Buddha's disciples are scattered now, but there still are five hundred disciples in the Buddha's presence. Please, O King, invite the Buddha to come to the city tomorrow. I shall make five hundred big elephants drunk. When the Buddha enters the city, I shall provoke the drunken elephants so that they will trample him to death and make an end to his kind. I shall be the Buddha instead and convert the world!" Upon hearing this, King Ajātaśatru was happy, and he immediately went to where the Buddha was. He kowtowed and did obeisance, and said to the Buddha: "Tomorrow I shall arrange for a modest gift. I would like humbly to invite you, World-honored One, and your disciples to a meal in my palace." The Buddha knew his plan and answered: "Excellent! We shall go tomorrow morning." The king withdrew and left. Upon his return he said to Devadatta: "The Buddha has accepted my invitation. In agreement with our previous plan you must make the elephants drunk. Look out and wait for him!" The next day at mealtime, the Buddha and his five hundred arhats entered the gate of the city. Five hundred drunken elephants came forward trumpeting. They rushed against the walls and knocked down the trees. People panicked and the whole city was terrified. The five hundred arhats flew up into the air. Only the Venerable Ānanda stayed by the Buddha's side while the drunk elephants all charged straight toward the Buddha. The Buddha merely raised his hand, and his five fingers appropriately changed to five lion kings. They all roared with the same voice and made heaven and earth tremble. Thereupon the drunk elephants bent their knees, fell to the ground, and did not dare raise their heads. Their intoxication then ended. They wept and felt remorse for their misdeed. The king and his subjects were all overawed. The World-honored One slowly came forward and arrived at the king's palace. After he had eaten with his arhats, he recited a formula. The king said to the Buddha: "My nature is not bright. I believed in calumny and I started doing evil. My scheme was not right. Please have great mercy and forgive me for my foolishness." Thereupon the World-honored One informed Ajātaśatru and the whole great multitude: "In the world there are eight things that increase slander, all stemming from fame. Furthermore, by coveting gain and 596b honors one brings about great sins, unending for eons. Which eight? Gain and loss, defamation and fame, praise and ridicule, suffering and pleasure. From olden times to the present one seldom is free from them." Thereupon the World-honored One spoke the stanzas:

> 1. People have been slandering each other from of old till now. They slander him who talks too much and they slander him who speaks slowly, and they also slander those who do neither. In the world there is none who is not slandered.

> 2. If one's intention is to revile the noble, one cannot decide equitably. Now slandering and now praising, it is merely for one's fame and gain.

3. The intelligent are eulogized. Yes, they are praised as proper and worthy. When a wise man keeps the precepts, he is not ridiculed.

4. No one is maligned who is as pure as an arhat. The gods admire him, and he is praised by Brahmā and Śakra.

After the Buddha had spoken the stanzas, he again informed the king: "Once there was a king who liked to eat the meat of wild geese. He used to dispatch a hunter to spread his nets and catch geese. The hunter presented a goose a day to provide for the king's meal. Then there was a goose king who flew down at the head of five hundred geese to seek for food. The goose king fell into the net and was caught by the hunter. The other geese kept flying about in consternation and did not leave. There was a particular goose who kept fluttering about and followed, without avoiding bows and arrows. It cried in a piteous way, spitting blood, never ceasing, day and night. When the hunter saw this righteous behavior, he felt compassion. He then set the goose king free, so that he might go with the others. When the flock of geese had reclaimed their king, they surrounded him full of joy. The hunter then told everything to the king. The king also sensed the righteous act and henceforth stopped catching geese." The Buddha informed King Ajātaśatru: "The goose king at that time is myself. The particular goose is the worthy Ānanda. The flock of five hundred geese are the present five hundred arhats. The king who ate geese is you now, great king. The hunter then is Devadatta now. Since his former existence he has constantly desired to harm me. Because of the power of my great compassion, he was saved. Disregarding his enmity, I have brought about my becoming a Buddha." When the Buddha explained this, the king and his ministers were all delighted.

Chapter XXVI

Defilements

Once there was a man without brothers. When he was a child his parents loved him dearly. They were compassionate and diligent, and wanted him to grow up perfect. They took him to teachers and urged him to study writing. But the child was arrogant and never paid any attention. He discarded in the evening what he had received in the morning. He did not remember anything. Thus it was for several years and he did not know anything. His parents called him back to let him manage the family's affairs. But their child was boastful and was not diligent in his endeavors. The family consequently became destitute and everything seemed to slip away. The son was heedless and did not care to keep any records, selling off family possessions. He was buoyant and did as he pleased. He let his hair become disheveled, went barefoot, and wore unclean clothes. He was stingy and impudent, and did not heed shame and disgrace. He was foolish, self-satisfied, and held in contempt by others. The people all detested him and they called him wicked. On his way in or out of the house, no one talked to him. He was not aware of his wickedness; on the contrary, he blamed everyone else. First of all he harbored resentment against his parents, and then he reproved his teachers: "The spirits of my ancestors are unwilling to help me. They let me weep even though I am in such dire straits. It would be better to serve the Buddha and be able to obtain merit." So he went to where the Buddha was and did obeisance. He came forward and said to the Buddha: "O Buddha, your Path is vast, and it does not exclude anyone. I wish to be your disciple. I beg to receive your permission." The Buddha

596c

informed him: "Well, if you want to seek for the Path, you must practice the pure ways. You bring common worldly taints if you enter my Path. You aimed at perfection in vain. How could you benefit? It would be better to return home and serve your parents with filial piety. Practice the instructions of your teachers and never forget them as long as you live! Diligently carrying out your affairs as a layman, you will prosper and be free from anxiety. Carry on with decency and do not commit any impropriety! Wash and dress up! Watch your words! Control your thoughts and keep them focused. If you mend your ways in the actions you undertake, and if you zealously practice them, you will be admired by others. Such conduct may be thought of as the Path!" Thereupon the World-honored One spoke the stanzas:

> 1. Non-recitation is a verbal taint. Want of diligence is a taint for the household. Want of dignity is a taint on appearance. Heedlessness is a taint of action.

> 2. Stinginess is a taint on charity. Unwholesomeness is a taint on conduct. In this world and the next, evil is always a taint.

> 3. As for the taint among taints, none is worse than foolishness. Reject it while applying yourself! Monk, be free from taints!

When the man had heard the stanzas, he understood his arrogance and foolishness. He accepted the Buddha's instructions and responded with joy. Reflecting upon the meaning of the stanzas, he repented and reformed. He served his parents with filial piety and respected his teachers. He studied the path of the scriptures and diligently conducted his affairs as a layman. He followed the precepts and kept control of himself. He did not do that which deviated from the Path. His relatives praised his filial piety and the people in the district praised his courtesy. His good name spread far and wide and within the land he was praised as a worthy. Three years later he went back to where the Buddha was. He fell prostrate in obeisance and he related in good faith: "My respect is utterly real and I have made my image complete. Rejecting evil and doing what is wholesome, I am congratulated by both high and low. Please, have great mercy! Let me be saved by practicing the Path!" When the Buddha said: "Welcome!", his hair fell off   597a and he immediately became an ascetic. Inwardly he reflected on tranquility and insight, the four truths, and the right path. As his zeal increased daily, he attained arhatship.

Chapter XXVII

The Righteous

Once there was an elder brahman called Satyaka Nirgrantha. His talents were distinct and he was very knowledgeable, the best in the land. He had five hundred disciples but he was haughty and proud of himself, without any regard for the world. He plated his belly with a sheet of iron. When someone asked him why, he said: "Because I am afraid my knowledge may overflow." When he heard that the Buddha had appeared in the world to convert people to the Path which has illuminated the world far and wide, he harbored jealousy and at no time was he at ease. He said to his disciples: "I hear that the ascetic Gautama calls himself a Buddha. I shall go now and ask him very profound and subtle questions that will make his heart palpitate and he will not know what to say." He immediately went with his disciples to the Jetavana and lined up outside the gate. From a distance they saw that the World-honored One's majestic splendor was as grand as the sun that has just risen. Their five feelings were aroused and their joy was mingled with fear. They then advanced to the front and did obeisance to the Buddha. The Buddha told him to sit. After they were seated, Nirgrantha asked the Buddha: "What is said to be a follower of the Path? What is said to be a learned one? What is said to be an elder? What is said to be an upright person? What is said to be an ascetic? What is said to be a monk? What is said to be a sage? What is said to be the attainment of the Path? What is said to be the maintenance of the precepts? If you can explain these to me, I wish to become your disciple." Thereupon the World-honored One contemplated the questions, and answered with the following stanzas:

1. One who is constantly compassionate and fond of study, who behaves with right thoughts and cherishes precious wisdom, he is said to be in the Path.

2. A so-called learned one is not necessarily eloquent. One who is without fear and apprehension, and guards what is wholesome, is a learned one.

3. One is not called an elder because of his advanced age. Although his appearance is mature and his hair white, he may just be foolish.

4. But one who cherishes the Doctrine of the truth, who is self-controlled and benevolent, and whose knowledge and understanding are pure, he is an elder.

5. One is called upright not when one is as beautiful as a flower, or is one who jealously covets vain ornaments and whose words differ from his conduct,

6. But who can discard evil after cutting off its roots, who is wise and without hatred, he is said to be upright.

7. A so-called ascetic is not necessarily someone who has taken the tonsure, while he continues to lie, covet, and desire like a common man.

8. But one who can stop evil and who expounds the Way extensively, calms his thoughts by extinguishing his bad intentions, he is said to be an ascetic.

9. A so-called monk is not someone who obtains his food by begging while he continues to aspire for salvation with wrong conduct and seek fame for its own sake.

10. But one who discards sinful actions and who purely practices clean living, whose wisdom enables him to destroy evil, he is a monk.

11. A so-called sage is not someone who does not speak while entertaining impure thoughts, only externally controlled.

597b

12. But one whose thoughts are unconditioned and whose internal behavior is pure, one who is tranquil here and everywhere, he is a sage.

13. A so-called possessor of the Path refers to someone who saves not a single being but the whole world, doing no harm in the Path.

14. When one is versed in the Doctrine, it does not mean he is eloquent. He may have little learning, but if he personally relies on his conduct according to the Doctrine, and if he keeps the Path and does not forget it, he is versed in the Doctrine.

When Satyaka Nirgrantha and his five hundred disciples heard these stanzas of the Buddha, they were delighted and their minds opened up. They rejected their haughtiness and all became ascetics. Nirgrantha alone manifested the mind of a bodhisattva, and his five hundred disciples all attained arhatship.

Chapter XXVIII

Practicing the Path

Once there was a brahman who had gone forth in his youth to study. Until the age of sixty, however, he was unable to obtain the Path. If at sixty one had not attained the Path, according to the rules of the brahmans, one should then return home, take a wife, and live at home. He had a son who was upright and lovely. At the age of seven he exhibited great intelligence in his study. He was eloquent and sometimes said things that were beyond people's grasp. Yet one day he suddenly fell gravely ill and his life ended. The brahman was stricken with grief and unable to cope with it. Exhausted, he fell prostrate on the corpse and when he rose again his relatives admonished him and took him away by force to prepare the corpse for burial outside the city. The brahman thought to himself: "I reckon that my weeping now will not do any good. It would be better to go to King Yamarāja and beg for my son's life." Thereupon the brahman cleansed himself, fasted, and offered flowers and incense. He left his house, and everywhere he went he asked: "Where is the place that King Yamarāja holds his court?" 597c He kept going for several thousands of *li*, and when he arrived deep in the mountains he saw brahmans who had attained the Path. When he asked them the same question, they in turn asked him: "What do you, sir, seek by asking about the place where King Yamarāja holds his court?" He answered: "I had a son who surpassed others in eloquence and wisdom. He suddenly passed away recently. I cannot get over my grief and vexation. I want to go to King Yamarāja to beg him for my son's life. I want to bring him back to his family and raise him, and prepare for my old age." The

155

brahmans felt sorry for his foolishness and informed him: "The place where King Yamarāja holds his court is not a place a living person can go to. We shall show you, sir, the right direction. If you go more than four hundred *li* westward from here, there is a large stream, and in it is a city. This is a city where divine spirits stay when they are on an inspection round in the world. King Yamarāja always makes his inspection round on the eighth day of the month, and he is sure to pass through this city. If you, sir, keep to the fasting prescriptions, you will certainly meet him when you go there." The brahman was delighted, and having received their instructions he went on his way. When he arrived by the stream, he saw a marvelous city. Its palaces and houses were like those of the Trāyastriṃśa gods. The brahman went to the gate, burned incense, raised his feet, and recited incantations, wanting to meet King Yamarāja. When King Yamarāja gave the order to meet and question him, the brahman stated: "At a late moment in my life I had a son and wanted to prepare for my old age. I brought him up for seven years, but recently his life ended. Please, great king, be merciful and generous! Give me back my child's life!" King Yamarāja said: "Your request is excellent! Your son, sir, is now disporting in the eastern garden. You may go there yourself to take him away." The brahman immediately went there and saw that his child was playing with other small children. He then went ahead, embraced him, and wept for him. He said: "While I was thinking of you night and day, my meals and sleep were not pleasant. Did you ever think of the suffering of your parents?" The small child was frightened and rebuked him, saying: "Foolish old man, you do not understand the way of reason. During his brief stay one may call someone a son. Do not speak any more vain words! It would be better for you to go quickly away! I momentarily have my own parents here. At this unexpected meeting your embrace has been in vain!" The brahman was disappointed and left in tears. He then thought: "I have heard that the ascetic Gautama knows how to transform man's spirit. I shall go and ask him." Thereupon the brahman returned to where the Buddha was. The Buddha then was in the Jetavana of Śrāvastī, expounding the Doctrine to his great multitude. When the brahman saw the Buddha, he kowtowed, did obeisance, and gave a full explanation of the circumstances to the Buddha: "He is truly my son, but he does not want to be called so. On the contrary, he says that I am a foolish old man. He acknowledged that he had been my son during his brief stay [but said that] we would never [again] have the feelings of father and son. Why is it so?" The Buddha informed the brahman: "You are really foolish. When someone dies, his spirit leaves and receives another form. Father and mother, wife and child, they come together because of certain circumstances, just like a guest who rises and departs. Bound by foolishness one still reckons them to be one's own. One does not recognize them as the basis of one's sorrow and distress. Immersed in the cycle of birth and death, one does not rest yet. Only the wise do not covet affection. He is aware of suffering but rejects its cause as such. He diligently cultivates the scriptural precepts. Since he has done away with any imaginings, his cycle of birth and death has ended." Thereupon the World-honored One spoke the stanzas:

598a

1. When a man cares for his wife and child but does not contemplate the principle of disease, death will come all of a sudden, just as quickly as swirling waters.

2. When a father and son are not saved, what hope would there be for other relatives? Relying on a relative when one's life has ended is like a blind man holding on to a torch.

3. When wisdom unravels such intention, one may perform the scriptural precepts. Diligently practicing to cross the world, one may completely remove suffering.

4. Stay far away from any abyss, just as the wind blows away the clouds. He who has extinguished his imaginings has insight.

5. Wisdom is best in the world. Satisfaction means the [realization of the] unconditioned nature. The wise one

receives the right teaching and ends the cycle of birth and death.

When the brahman heard the stanzas, he suddenly understood. He knew that life was impermanent and that wife and child are just like transient guests. He kowtowed and made an obeisance. Upon his wish to become an ascetic the Buddha said: "Excellent!" His hair fell off of itself and he donned the robe of the Doctrine. He immediately became a monk. By reflecting on the meaning of the stanzas, he extinguished his craving and did away with any imaginings. There on his seat he attained arhatship.

Chapter XXIX

Miscellaneous

Once the Buddha was in Śrāvastī, expounding the Doctrine and making conversions. Gods and dragons, demons and spirits, and the ruler and the people went to listen at three moments. The king at this time was called Prasenajit. As a man he was arrogant and given to pleasure. His eyes were deluded by lust, and his ears were confused by sounds. His nose was attracted to fragrances, his mouth was unrestrained about the five flavors, and his body was conditioned to subtle, smooth things. His food and drink were extremely fine, but he never had enough of them. So food was often presented to him, as he was constantly suffering from hunger. The delicacies of his kitchen did not satiate his constant hunger. He became fat, unable to ride in a carriage. Whether lying down or standing up, he was indeed short of breath. His breath was obstructed and his breathing interrupted, which constantly 598b alarmed him. He was groaning whether sitting or standing, and constantly suffered from the weight of his own body. He could not turn aside. He considered his body to be a calamity. So he ordered a stately chariot and went to where the Buddha was. While his attendants supported him, he made inquiries, withdrew, and sat down, his hands folded together. He said to the Buddha: "World-honored One, from a great distance I have humbly come to visit you, asking your counsel free from any procedure. I do not know what my crime is that my body has become so bloated. I myself cannot perceive why I have become so. I constantly suffer from it. That is the reason why I have neglected to visit you more often."
The Buddha informed the great king: "There are five things that

159

make a person corpulent. One, frequent meals; two, fondness for sleep; three, merriment; four, absence of grief; five, uneventfulness. These are the five things, and being fond of them makes one corpulent. If one does not want to be corpulent, one will become lean, having diminished one's food, not caring for it." Thereupon the World-honored One spoke the stanza:

> 1. One must always be mindful! At each meal, know
> frugality! Accordingly, one's painful needs will diminish.
> Moderation preserves life.

When the king heard the stanza, his joy was immeasurable. He immediately called his cook and informed him: "Accept the recitation of this stanza! At mealtime, expound the stanza to me before serving the meal!"

The king took his leave and returned to the palace. When the cook offered a meal, he forthwith expounded the stanza. When the king heard the stanza he was glad, and he diminished his meal a spoonful each day. As his meals diminished little by little, his body consequently became lighter and he eventually became as lean as before. When he saw his condition, he was happy and remembered the Buddha. So he stood up, walked to where the Buddha was, and did obeisance. The Buddha told him to sit down, and asked the king: "Your horses and carriage and your followers are in their usual condition now. Why did you come on foot?" The king was glad to say to the Buddha: "The instructions, O Buddha, that I received have been carried out as I should. I have become lighter now through your power, World-honored One. That is why I have come on foot. You know what is best." The Buddha informed the great king: "People in the world are so ignorant about impermanence! They keep desiring all their lives long, not thinking about performing merits. When someone has died, the spirit leaves and the body remains in the grave. The wise nurture their spirits and the foolish ones nurture their bodies. If you can understand this, then respectfully carry out the noble teaching!" Thereupon the World-honored One again spoke the stanzas:

2. As man is impermanent, he ages as does an ox. He just grows and becomes fatter, without any wisdom.

3. Birth and death are wearisome, and coming and going are distressing. As one intently covets the body, one experiences unending suffering.

4. The wise know suffering, and thereby reject the body. They extinguish bad thoughts and do away with desire. When their craving has ended, they are free from rebirth.

When the king had heard the stanzas, he was glad and readily understood the meaning. He then became intent on starting on the unsurpassed right Path. Those who had been listening were countless, and they all gained the eye of the Doctrine.

[The section (T.599b18–599c18) has been moved to this location (between T.598b29 and T.598b1).]

Once there were seven monks who went into the mountains to apply themselves to the Path. After twelve years they could not obtain the Path. They talked it over among themselves and said: "Application to the Path is very difficult. We ruin the body as we restrain ourselves. We cannot avoid the hardship of the cold. All our life we have been begging for our food and the shame experienced is hard to endure. We finally could not obtain the Path. Our wrongdoings are difficult to do away with. We have been toiling in vain, perishing in the mountains. It would be better to return home and start a new family, to marry and raise children. Let us undertake some profitable business, be cheerful and happy. How can we know what comes later!" Thereupon the seven persons rose and left the mountains. From a distance the Buddha knew that they should be saved. Unable to bear some small suffering, they would finally fall into hell. Very, very sad! So the Buddha transformed himself into an ascetic, went to the valley, and met the seven monks. The transformed man said: "You have undertaken application to the Path for a long time. Why do you leave?" The seven men answered: "Our application to the Path has been painstaking, but the root of wrongdoing is hard to eradicate. We have begged for food on our alms rounds. The shame we have experienced was hard to endure. There was nobody who worshiped us in these mountains. We have been restless for many years, always guarding our frugality. Our distress has been in vain. The Path could not be obtained. We just want to return home and strive for amply profitable undertakings. We shall amass great wealth. Later, when old, we shall seek the Path." The transformed ascetic said: "Just stop! Stop! Listen to what I have to say! Man's life is impermanent. Even a day is not guaranteed. Application to the Path may be difficult, but after the initial suffering comes happiness. Living in a home is hard, without rest for a hundred thousand eons. Staying together with wife and children, one wishes to share peace and gains. One's aspiration is for everlasting happiness and not to meet with any calamity. This is like curing an illness by taking poison. You will make it worse, not better. All who appear in the three worlds know sorrow. Only if one is devout and not heedless concerning the precepts, and if one zealously strives to obtain the Path, will all suffering forever end." Thereupon the transformed ascetic manifested the characteristics of the Buddha. His radiant appearance was imposing and he thus spoke the stanzas:

599c

> 5. Application is hard and so is the eradication of wrongdoing. Living in a home is hard too. Staying together and sharing gains is hard. There is nothing harder than existence.

> 6. Monks, begging is hard. How could it be possible not to exert oneself! Through strenuous pursuit, obtainment comes naturally, and in the end there will be no desire in man.

> 7. If one has faith, one's precepts will be realized. Through faith one brings about a great number of precious things. Also through this, one gains harmony. Wherever one may be, one is worshiped.

8. Now sitting and then lying down in a place, if one's whole conduct is not negligent and if one keeps the unity and maintains a proper mind, one is certain to be happy, dwelling among the trees.

Thereupon, when the seven monks had seen the characteristics of the Buddha's person, and had furthermore heard these stanzas, they were mortified and awestruck. They fell prostrate in obeisance and kowtowed at the Buddha's feet. Collecting their thoughts and repenting their error, they did obeisance and went away. They returned to the mountains and were zealous in conduct until death. Reflecting on the meaning of the stanzas, they kept their unity and proper mind. Dwelling in the forest they attained quietude and gained arhatship.

Chapter XXX

Hell

In the land of Śrāvastī there was once a brahman teacher called Pūraṇa Kāśyapa. He had a following of five hundred disciples. No one, whether the king or the people, failed to wait on him. The Buddha had recently attained the Path and arrived in Śrāvastī from Rājagṛha with his disciples. His personal appearance was brilliant and the instructions of his Path were lucid. The king and his court and the people in the whole territory all respected him. Thereupon Pūraṇa Kāśyapa became jealous and wanted to destroy the World-honored One. He expected to be respectfully served all alone. So he led his disciples to meet with King Prasenajit and made a plea: "We elders have applied ourselves to the old teachers of the land. The ascetic Gautama has appeared later in search of the Path. Although, in reality, there is nothing divine about him, he calls himself the Buddha. Yet you, O King, forsake me and want to serve only him. Now I would like to probe the qualities of the Path with the Buddha and to know who will be victorious. May you, O King, serve the winner all your life!" The king said: "Very well!" So the king went to where the Buddha was in his majestic carriage. Having greeted him, he informed him: "Pūraṇa Kāśyapa wants to thoroughly test the power of the Path with you, World-honored One. I wonder if you, World-honored One, would agree." The Buddha said: "Excellent! After a period of seven days I shall test his transformation." The king installed two high seats in a fine place in the wide plain east of the city. They were forty *chang* (the equivalent of four hundred feet) high and adorned with the seven precious things. He made a display of pendant streamers and adjusted the seats. The distance between the two seats was two *li*, and the disciples of the two schools sat below them. The whole population, including the king and his ministers, gathered there. They wanted to watch the two men probing each other's divine transformation. Thereupon Pūraṇa Kāśyapa and his disciples arrived first at his seat and he was about to climb the steps. A demon king called Pāñcika saw Kāśyapa's vain jealousy and raised a big storm, blowing at his high seat. His seating turned over and the pendant streamers flew about. It rained sand and shingles, and their eyes were blinded.

Meanwhile, the high seat of the World-honored One was stable and did not move at all; the Buddha and his great multitude came in a solemn way and they directed themselves toward the high seat. After he had mounted it, straightaway the whole community of monks quietly sat down. The king and his ministers kowtowed even more respectfully and they informed the Buddha: "Please, confer your divine transformation, suppress our wrong views, and let the people in the land clearly hold faith in what is right and true!" Thereupon the World-honored One all of a sudden was not visible on his seat. He ascended in the air and emitted a vast light. He disappeared in the east and became visible in the west, and this applied as well to the four directions. His person emitted water and fire. He was up and down alternatively. Sitting and lying in the air, he made twelve more transformations. Making himself disappear and making himself invisible, he returned to his seat. Gods, dragons, and demons and spirits worshiped him with flowers and incense. Their voices of praise shook heaven and earth. Pūraṇa Kāśyapa knew there was no way out. He hung his head down in shame and did not dare lift up his eyes. Thereupon the adamantine hero raised his adamantine bolt, and fire came from the tip of the bolt. He pointed it at Kāśyapa [and said]: "Why do you not show your transformation, sir?" Kāśyapa was terrified. He abandoned his seat and left; his five hundred disciples also removed themselves and scattered. The majestic countenance of the World-honored One did not delight them in their distress. He returned to the Jetavana, to the garden of Anāthapiṇḍada. On the other hand, the king and his ministers were very happy and withdrew. In consequence, Pūraṇa Kāśyapa and his disciples went away in disgrace. On their way they met an aged *upāsikā* by the name of Mo-ni. She railed against them: "You bunch of fools, you did not reflect enough! You still wanted to compare with the Buddha, probing the qualities of his Path! You fools and impostors, you do not have any sense of shame! You must not walk in the world with such a face!" Pūraṇa Kāśyapa was ashamed for his disciples. When they reached the bank of a river, he lied to his disciples: "When I throw myself into the water now, I shall certainly be reborn in the brahma heaven. If I do not return, know that I am happy there!" His disciples waited for him, but he did not return. They discussed among themselves: "Our master has certainly gone to heaven. Why should we stay?" One by one they threw themselves into the water, hoping to follow their master. Unknowingly led by their wrongdoing, they all fell into hell. Later, when the king heard about the event, he was quite startled and felt uncanny. He went to where the Buddha was and inquired: "Why did master Pūraṇa Kāśyapa and his followers err so?" The Buddha informed the king: "Master Pūraṇa Kāśyapa and his followers did two serious wrongdoings: one, while still immersed in the three poisons, they praised themselves for having attained the Path; two, by slandering the Tathāgata, they expected to be treated with respect. Because of these two wrongdoings, they had to fall into hell. They were prompted by their misfortune and threw themselves into the river. Their bodies have died and their spirits have departed, but the suffering they experience is immeasurable. That is why a wise one controls his thoughts. Internally, he does not engender what is unwholesome, and externally, evil does not arise. When for instance a frontier town is in contact with bandits, there is nothing to fear if the defense is solid. People inside are safe and the bandits outside cannot come in. A wise one guards himself in the same way." Thereupon the World-honored One spoke the stanzas:

1. He who by false assumptions seeks a bribe, whose actions have not been correct, who finds fault with good people, and who administers the world on the basis of false accusations, such a man, led on by his own wrongdoing, throws himself into a pit.

2. As in defending a frontier town, [one must] be firm both outside and inside, just so guard your thoughts! What is wrong will not arise! If, however, one's actions are deficient, one brings on sorrow, causing one to eventually fall into hell.

599b

After the Buddha had spoken the stanzas, he again informed the king: "A long time ago there were two monkey kings, each heading five hundred monkeys. One king became jealous and wanted to kill the other king. He schemed to rule all alone, and went on the attack. He repeatedly failed, however, and retreated in shame. He arrived at the shore of a great sea. In a bay there was a heap of foam on the water, and as the wind was blowing, it was piling up, several hundred *chang* (thousand feet) high. In his foolishness the monkey king thought it was the Snowy Mountain and he said to his group: 'I have long heard that there is a great Snowy Mountain in the sea. In it one is happy and sweet fruits are pleasant to the mouth. Today I have seen it. I shall go first and have a look. If it is clearly pleasant, I will not return. If it is not pleasant, I will return and tell you.' Thereupon he climbed in a tree and jumped with all his strength. He threw himself into the heap of foam and sank to the bottom of the sea. The others wondered why he did not come out. They thought he was certainly very happy and jumped in one by one, thus depleting the group in drowning." The Buddha informed the king: "The jealous monkey king at that time was the present Pūraṇa Kāśyapa. The group was Pūraṇa Kāśyapa's present five hundred disciples. That other monkey king was myself. Because Pūraṇa Kāśyapa was involved with jealousy in his earlier existence, led on by his wrongdoing he threw himself into a heap of foam, bringing an end to his group and depleting his kind. He has now slandered me again and they have all jumped into the river. The retribution for his evil will make him burn for eons without any limit." When the king heard this, he gained pious understanding. He did obeisance and left.

Chapter XXXI

Similes with the Elephant

Once, when Rāhula had not yet attained the Path, his nature was rude and his words untrustful. The Buddha ordered Rāhula: "Go to Āmrayaṣṭikā and stay in its pure abode! Guard your mouth, control your mind, and diligently develop the scriptural precepts!" Rāhula accepted the instructions, did obeisance, and left. He stayed there for ninety days and felt shame and regret. He could not rest night or day. When the Buddha went to see him, Rāhula was very glad. He rushed forward and greeted the Buddha. He arranged a rope bed and adjusted his *cīvara* (upper robe). The Buddha occupied the rope bed and told Rāhula: "Take some water with your washing bowl and wash my feet for me!" Rāhula accepted the instruction and washed the Buddha's feet. When it was done, the Buddha said to Rāhula: "Do you see the water to wash the feet in the washing bowl?" Rāhula said to the Buddha: "Indeed, I see it!" The Buddha said to Rāhula: "Can one use this water for food and drink, to wash the hands, or to rinse the mouth?" Rāhula said: "One must not use it again. Why? This water was originally clean, but having washed your feet it is defiled now. That is why one must not use it again." The Buddha said to Rāhula: "The same applies to you. Even though you are my son and the grandson of the king, even though you have given up worldly splendor and emoluments to become an ascetic, you do not pay attention to strenuous pursuit while controlling your thoughts and guarding your mouth. The impurity of the three poisons fills your feelings, just like this water which cannot be used again." The Buddha further said to Rāhula: "Throw away the water in the washing bowl!"

600a

Rāhula immediately threw it away, and the Buddha said to Rāhula: "Even though the washing bowl is empty, may one not fill it again with food and drink?" He said: "One must not! Why? Because it is known as a washing bowl that has been defiled." The Buddha said to Rāhula: "The same applies to you. Even though you are an ascetic, your mouth is not trustworthy. Your disposition is overbearing and you do not pay attention to strenuous pursuit. You have a bad reputation, just like the washing bowl that must not be filled up with food." The Buddha kicked away the washing bowl with his toes, and it rolled of its own accord, jumping away several times before it stopped. The Buddha said to Rāhula: "Would you be careful with this washing bowl, afraid it might break?" Rāhula informed the Buddha: "A basin to wash the feet is something cheap. Even if one were to care for it, one will not be particularly attentive." The Buddha said to Rāhula: "The same applies to you. Even though you are an ascetic, you do not control your body and mouth. Many are injured by your harsh words. You are not loved by the multitude and the wise do not cherish you. When your body dies and your spirit leaves, you will be twisting in the three woeful destinations. As you are born and die, your suffering will be immeasurable, not pitied by any Buddha or noble one, just as you said not to care for the washing bowl." When Rāhula heard this, he felt shame and fear. The Buddha informed Rāhula: "Let me explain it with a simile. Once a king had a huge elephant who was fierce and keen in battle. His strength was superior to that of any of the five hundred smaller elephants. That king raised an army and wanted to attack an opposing country. He dressed up the elephant with iron armor, and assigned an elephant master to control it. He tied a couple of halberds to the two teeth of the elephant. He also attached two double-edged swords to his two ears and tied curved swords to the four legs of the elephant. He furthermore attached iron cudgels to the elephant's tail and covered the elephant with nine weapons, all of which were extremely sharp. The elephant just hid his trunk, guarding it and did not use it to fight. The elephant master was glad, knowing that the elephant was protecting his life. Why? An elephant's trunk is soft, and if it is hit by an arrow the elephant will die. That is why he did not thrust his trunk in a fight. When the elephant had been fighting for a long time, however, he would thrust his trunk looking for a sword. 600b The elephant master did not like it because he thought that this fierce elephant did not have any regard for his own life. Thrusting his trunk looking for a sword, he wanted to hold it with the tip of his trunk. The king and his ministers were concerned about this huge elephant and they decided not to let him fight again." The Buddha informed Rāhula: "Men commit nine evils, but they merely have to guard their mouth, just as this huge elephant guarded its trunk and did not fight. Why so? He was afraid to be hit by an arrow and die. That is why man likewise guards his mouth. He must fear the three woeful destinations and the suffering in hell. If he commits all ten evils and does not guard his mouth, he might lose his life like this huge elephant who thrust its trunk in a fight, not counting on being hit by an arrow! The same applies to man when all ten evils are committed and he does not reflect on the three woeful destinations and the suffering of the poisons. If however he performs the ten wholesome actions, controls his body, mouth, and mind, and commits no evil, he may obtain the Path and be free from the three destinations and the calamity of repeating the cycle of birth and death." Thereupon the World-honored One spoke the stanzas:

> 1. I fight like an elephant, unafraid of a hit by an arrow. With trustworthiness I shall save [even] people without moral precepts.

> 2. When for instance an elephant is tame, it may be mounted by a king. A well-regulated person is most respected and is bestowed trust.

When Rāhula heard the earnest admonitions of the Buddha, he was moved and encouraged. He remembered them and did not forget. He was full of zeal but mild, and his forbearance was like the earth. His imaginings quieted down and he attained the path of the arhat.

Once the Buddha was in the pure abode of the Jetavana in the land of Śrāvastī, proclaiming the great Doctrine to the disciples of the four divisions, to gods, dragons, and spirits, and to the ruler and his subjects. At that time there was an elder layman called Ho-t'i-t'an (Hastidamaka?). He came to where the Buddha was, did obeisance to the Buddha, withdrew, and sat aside. He folded his hands, knelt deeply and said to the World-honored One: "I have long been receiving your great teaching, looking up to you and serving you, but under the pressure of personal matters I have been incapable. Please be merciful!" The World-honored One had him take a seat and asked him where he had come from and his name. He knelt deeply and answered: "Actually I am a kind of lay disciple. My name is Hastidamaka, and at the time of the former king I was the king's elephant tamer." The Buddha asked the layman how many principles are necessary in taming elephants, and he replied: "I always tame a big elephant by using three things. Which three? One, a firm hook. I hold its mouth with it and place the reins. Two, by diminishing its food I always let it grow lean. Three, I lash it with a rod, making it feel pain. With these three things I can tame it well." The Buddha further asked: "When applying these three things, what is it you control?" "When I hold its mouth with an iron hook, I thereby restrain its strength. When I do not give it sufficient food and drink, I restrain its fierceness of body. If I give it a beating with a rod, I subdue its mind. That is the right way to tame it." "If you have subdued it, what can you use it for?" He replied: "If it is subdued, it may be mounted by a king, and one may let it fight. It will advance or retreat as you wish, without resistance." The Buddha further asked the lay disciple: "Is there just this method? Isn't there anything else?" He replied: "To tame an elephant, there is just this way!" The Buddha informed the lay disciple: "You can only tame an elephant. You must further be able to tame yourself!" So he said: "I wonder what taming oneself may mean? Please, World-honored One, teach me what has not yet been made known!" The Buddha informed the lay disciple: "I also have three things by which I subdue everyone,

600c

and by means of subduing oneself, one gains access to the realm of the unconditioned. One, control one's verbal actions in utmost sincerity. Two, suppress one's corporeal vigor through pure compassion. Three, extinguish one's cover of mental foolishness through wisdom. With these three things one may be delivered from everything, be free from the three woeful destinations, realize the unconditioned, and not experience any sorrow or suffering caused by the cycle of birth and death." Thereupon the World-honored One spoke the stanzas:

> 3. An elephant like the one called Dhanapālaka is fierce and hard to restrain. It may be reined in and not given food, but it is still a very wild elephant.

> 4. Basically, my mind's actions are pure, and it always acts in contentment. I have completely rejected its fetters and regulated it like an elephant restrained by a hook.

> 5. If one finds happiness in the Path and is not negligent, and if one can always guard his thoughts, one may pull himself out of corporeal suffering, just like an elephant leaving a pitfall.

> 6. Although one is always well trained like the Sindhu (horses) or the fine elephants, it would be better to be self-disciplined.

> 7. He is unable to go there, nor can others do it. Only one who disciplines himself can reach the plane of the self-disciplined.

When the lay disciple heard the stanzas, his joy was immeasurable. He understood deep inside, and immediately attained the eye of the Doctrine. Those who were listening were countless, and they all attained the Path.

Chapter XXXII

Craving

Once the Buddha was in the land of Rājagṛha, in a pure abode on Mount Gṛdhrakūṭa, expounding the great Doctrine for gods and men and for dragons and spirits. Then there was a man who had left his family, his wife and child, and who came to where the Buddha was. He did obeisance to the Buddha and asked to be an ascetic. The Buddha immediately accepted him as an ascetic. He instructed him to sit underneath a tree and reflect on the qualities of the Path. Having received his instructions, the monk went deep into the mountains, more than a hundred *li* from the pure abode. 601a He sat alone among the trees and reflected on the Path for three years, but his thoughts were not firm and he wanted to return. He thought that to leave his family in search of the Path was difficult and it would be better to return quickly to see his wife and child. After he thought thus, he rose and left the mountains.

With his noble penetrating insight, the Buddha saw that this monk deserved to obtain the Path, that he was returning because of his foolishness. With his supernatural power the Buddha transformed himself into an ascetic. He went in the opposite direction and they met along the way. The transformed person asked where he came from. "This place is flat. Let us sit down and talk." Thereupon the two men sat down and talked at ease. He then answered the transformed man's question: "I left my family, my wife and child, wanting to be an ascetic, but dwelling deep in these mountains I could not obtain the Path. Separation from my wife and child may not be as good as I had hoped. I have been wasting away my life in vain. I have not obtained anything by toiling. Now I want

177

to return, feeling sorry, and see my wife and child. We shall readily enjoy ourselves and later make plans again." All of a sudden there appeared an old monkey who had left the forest. He was in a place without any trees and living there. The transformed ascetic asked the monk: "Why is this monkey all alone on the plains? There are no trees. How does he enjoy himself?" The monk replied to the transformed person: "I have been seeing this monkey for a long time. He has come to live here for two reasons. Which two? One, because of his wife and child and many relatives, he could not obtain sufficient food and drink, but it was his joy to give full rein to his mouth. Two, night and day he constantly went up and down the trees so that the soles of his feet were worn down and he could not find any rest. For these two reasons he left the trees to come and live here." At the moment the two men were talking, they again saw the monkey going away and returning to the trees. The transformed ascetic said to the monk: "Did you see the monkey go back to the trees?" He answered: "I have. This animal is foolish. He left the trees, but then enters them again, while his group remains restive, and he is not wearied with the trouble." The transformed man said: "The same applies to you, sir. What is the difference [between you and] this monkey! For two reasons you, sir, have come and entered these mountains. Which two? [One,] because your wife and dwelling were a prison. Two, because your child and relatives were shackles. That is why you, sir, have come in search of the Path to end the suffering attendant on birth and death. Now you want to return to your family, to renew your shackles and reenter the prison. Love and affection [ironically] lead straight to hell." The transformed ascetic, 1.6 *chang* (sixteen feet) tall, then showed his primary and secondary marks. His golden light shining everywhere, he moved the whole mountain. Flying birds and running animals came looking for the light. They all recognized their former lives and deeply repented their misdeeds. Thereupon the World-honored One spoke the stanzas:

1. When, for instance, the roots of a tree are very firm, although it is cut down it will still grow again. If one's

craving mind is not completely done away with, one will soon experience suffering again.

2. Like a monkey who has left the trees but who, although delivered, hastens back to the trees, such acts are repeated by people. Having left their prison they reenter it.

3. A covetous mind is a constant stream. Its practices are accompanied by arrogance. When one's imaginings are set on desire, one is covered [by its elements] and does not see anything.

4. While all intentions are widely flowing and the fetter of craving acts like a creeper, one can eradicate the root of the intentions only by perceiving them distinctly through wisdom.

5. Now, as craving is lush, notions are its tendrils. When covetousness is deep, without bottom, [the travails of] old age and death will increase through it.

When the monk saw the brightness of the Buddha's light and heard the words of the stanzas, he was struck with fear. He fell prostrate in obeisance, confessed his sin, and apologized for his misdeed. Internally, he immediately removed himself, counted his breath, and, as a result of his tranquility and insight, attained arhatship in front of the Buddha. All the gods had come to listen, and they were all glad. They scattered flowers and worshiped, and their praises [of him] were immeasurable.

Volume Four

Chapter XXXII

(*continued*)

Once, when the Buddha was in the land of Śrāvastī, expounding the Doctrine to gods and men, there was a brahman elder in the city whose wealth was immeasurable. He was stingy and not fond of giving. He used to close the gate during meals and did not like to have guests. When it was mealtime he would order his gatekeeper to close the doors firmly and not let anyone enter the gate unless he had a good reason. When begging or asking for something, an ascetic or a brahman could not gain entry to see him. The elder would immediately think of nice food, and order his wife to prepare food and drink. He instructed her to kill a plump chicken, blend it with ginger and pepper, and broil it. An arrangement of dishes was made on the spot, and he ordered that the outside gate be closed. Husband and wife both sat down and their small child was placed in the middle. In this way, they drank and ate together. The parents took the chicken meat and fed the child. They did this a number of times and did not abandon the practice. The Buddha knew that this elder's former merit should save him, and so he transformed himself into an ascetic. Watching while they sat down eating, he appeared in front of their seats. He uttered incantations and further mentioned that with some giving, one could obtain great merit. When the elder raised his head and saw the transformed ascetic, he immediately scolded him, saying: "You may be a man of the Path, but you are shameless. Why do you give offense while I sit eating with my household?" The ascetic answered: "You, sir, are foolish. You do not know any shame! I am a beggar. Why would I be ashamed?" The elder asked: "I and my household, we are enjoying ourselves. Why would I be ashamed?" The ascetic replied: "You have killed your father and married your mother, and you worship your enemy, not knowing any shame. But you say to me, a beggar, how shameful I am!" Thereupon the ascetic spoke the stanzas:

> 6. The sprouting creeper is not cut off, and yet you just keep enjoying your desire for food. You feed your enemy and augment the tombs. A foolish person is always pressed.

> 7. In a prison there may be hooks and irons, but a wise person does not consider them to be a prison. When a fool sees the adornments of wife and child, his mind is firmly attached to them.

> 8. The wise explain craving as a prison, very solid and difficult to leave. Therefore, sever from it! Do not see desire as bringing happiness!

When the elder heard these stanzas, he was startled, and asked earnestly: "Man of the Path, why do you expound these words?" The man of the Path answered: "The chicken on your table was your father in a previous existence. Because of his stinginess he was constantly reborn among chickens to be eaten by you, sir. This small child was a flesh-eating devil (*rākṣasa*), and you, sir, were a trader. Your father had boarded a ship and gone to sea. A sudden current shipwrecked him in the land of the *rākṣasa*s, and he was eaten by a *rākṣasa*. And so, when his life ended after five hundred existences, the *rākṣasa* came to be your son, sir. Because your remaining evil is not over yet, he came with the intention to harm you. Your present wife was your mother in a previous existence, sir. Because her love was so strong, she now is your wife still. You are foolish now and you do not know your previous lives. You killed your father and fed your enemy, and you have taken your mother

602b

as your wife. The wheel of birth and death in the five destinations turns without end. Going round in the five destinations, who can know? Only a man of the Path sees this world and observes the other. A fool does not know. How would he not be ashamed!" Thereupon the elder's hair was suddenly standing on end and he was terrified. The Buddha manifested his awesome supernatural power and revealed to him his former lives. When the elder saw the Buddha, he immediately recognized his former lives. He subsequently repented, apologized to the Buddha, and accepted the five precepts. The Buddha expounded the Doctrine to him, and he immediately became a stream-enterer.

Once the Buddha was in the Jetavana in Śrāvastī, expounding the Doctrine. There was a young monk then who had gone to the city on his alms round. He saw a young woman whose beauty was beyond compare. His thoughts kept longing for her. Bound by delusion, he could not free himself. He then fell ill and could not eat or drink. His appearance was haggard and he just lay down without getting up. When the men of the Path who were his fellows in study went to ask him what was ailing him, the young monk explained all that was on his mind. "I want to do away with my thoughts of the Path and follow my craving, but my wish is not fulfilled. I am sick with grief." His fellow students reproved him, but it did not enter his ears. So they forced him and helped him to go to where the Buddha was. They reported the whole matter to the World-honored One. The Buddha informed the young monk: "Your wish is easy to obtain. It is not worth any grief. I shall expediently solve this for you. Stand up and eat and drink!" When the monk heard this, he gained confidence and was glad, and his sadness was immediately over. Then the World-honored One led this monk and his great multitude to the city of Śrāvastī, to the home of the beautiful woman. The woman had died and they had laid her corpse out for three days. Her household was in mourning and could not stand to bury her. Her body was putrid and swollen, with impurities flowing out. The Buddha informed the monk: "The beautiful woman you were longing for is now like this. Everything is impermanent. Change comes within a breath. A fool contemplates the outside and does not see the ugly side. He thinks falsely that being entangled in the net of sin brings happiness." Thereupon the World-honored One spoke the stanzas:

> 9. Seeing beauty the mind is fascinated. It does not reflect on seeing it as impermanent. The fool considers what is beautiful to be good. How would he know that this is untrue!

> 10. [The fool] likes to be wrapped up in lust, like a silkworm weaving a cocoon. The wise one is able to give it up. Without ogling, he removes all suffering.

> 11. One whose thoughts are loose sees lust as pure. His craving mind increases and he consequently builds his own prison.

> 12. He who awakens his mind and destroys his lust always thinks that desire is impure, and he consequently leaves his evil prison. He can do away with the calamities of old age and death.

602c

Thereupon, when the young monk saw that this woman had been dead for three days, that her countenance was swollen and rotting, and that the stench was hard to approach, and when he further heard the stanzas with the World-honored One's pure instructions, he was sorry and his mind opened up. He knew he had been wrong. He did obeisance to the Buddha, kowtowed, and repented his error. He took refuge in the Buddha and was led back to the Jetavana. Throughout his life he was full of zeal, and he attained arhatship. When the countless people in the crowd understood that the desire for beauty was impure, their belief in the nature of impermanence was confirmed. Their coveting minds ceased and they attained the Path.

Once the Buddha was in a pure abode of Śrāvastī, expounding the Doctrine to gods, people, and dragons. There was an elder there whose wealth was immeasurable. He had a son, twelve or thirteen years of age. When his parents died, he was young and did not know about livelihood and how to manage the affairs of the family. He wasted the riches and within a few years they were gone. He went begging some time after, but he still could not provide for himself. His father had a relative, an elder whose great riches were immeasurable. One day the elder met him and he asked him about his circumstances. The elder took pity on him, took him back with him, and regulated everything. He gave him his daughter in marriage and provided him with servants, carriages, and horses. His riches were countless. He further built a residence and established a family. But as a man he was lazy. He did not keep any accounts and could not provide for their livelihood. Squandering and depleting his wealth, they were more distressed by hunger every day. Because of his daughter the elder gave him more riches, but he squandered them as before. They consequently became destitute. The elder frequently gave him money, but he used it recklessly. Thinking that he could not get any result, he wanted to take the wife away and marry her to another. While he was talking it over with his kindred, the daughter overheard them and went back to tell her husband: "My family is powerful and can take me away from you because you cannot provide a living. What will you do? What plan will you make?" When he heard his wife's words, he felt shame and thought to himself: "Yes, my merit is meager and I am full of mistakes. I am not versed in the ways of a family livelihood or of making a living. I am going to lose my wife now and I shall be begging, just as before. After love one becomes covetous. We shall part with life. How shall I cope with it!" He reflected and reflected and then he had an evil idea. He led his wife into their chamber and said: "I now want to die with you in the same place." He stabbed his wife on the spot and then stabbed himself. Both were dead. The slaves panicked and ran to inform 603a their elder. The elder and the young and old were alarmed, and when they came to have a look, they confirmed that they were dead. A funeral was held with their coffins and shrouds, as was the established custom in the land. The elder and the young and old were filled with grief. They kept thinking about the woman and did not leave. A while later, the elder heard that the Buddha was in the world converting and expounding the Doctrine, and that those who saw him were very glad, as they forgot their sorrow and did away with their distress. He thus led the family, young and old, to where the Buddha was. They did obeisance to the Buddha, withdrew, and sat aside. The Buddha asked the elder where he came from. "Why are you so sad and unhappy?" The elder said: "My house is unfortunate. I gave my only daughter in marriage, but she happened to meet a foolish husband who could not provide for a livelihood. When I wanted to take away his wife, he killed his wife and himself. They both died there. So we gave them a funeral. On our way back, we come to visit you, World-honored One." The Buddha informed the elder: "Covetousness and wrath are constant ailments in the world. Foolishness and ignorance are the gate to calamity. One falls into the abyss of the three realms and the five predestinations because of them. One keeps turning in the birth and death cycle for countless eons. One experiences every suffering, but still one does not repent. How much less could a foolish man realize this! The poison of covetousness destroys the self and one's family. It even harms all beings, *a fortiori* man and wife." Thereupon the World-honored One spoke the stanzas:

13. The fool binds himself with his covetousness, and he does not seek to cross to the other shore. He longs for riches, hurting others and himself too.

14. A mind that desires is a field in which lust, hatred, and delusion are the seeds. Therefore, when one gives to him who has passed beyond worldly things, the merits obtained are immeasurable.

15. When associates are few but goods numerous, a merchant is frightened and afraid. Exploiting his emotions,

bandits will harm his life. That is why the wise do not
covet anything.

Then, when the elder heard the Buddha's exposition of the stanzas,
he was delighted and happy. He forgot his sorrow and removed his
distress. Still in their seats, young and old, and all who were listening, destroyed their two million evil misdeeds and attained the path
of the stream-enterer.

Once the Buddha was in a pure abode in Śrāvastī expounding the
Doctrine to gods, dragons, spirits, and the ruler and his subjects.
Then there were two wandering fellows who were very good friends.
They always followed each other and did things together as if they
were one, without any difference. The two men deliberated and
decided that they wanted to be ascetics. They both went to where
the Buddha was, did obeisance, knelt deeply, and folded their
hands. They said to the Buddha: "We wish to be ascetics. Do give
us your permission!" The Buddha accepted them and they then
became ascetics. The Buddha ordered them to stay together in
one room. While the two were staying together, they just thought
of worldly desires and pleasures. Again and again they sighed for
sensuous appearances. Talking about their seductive exploits, they
were totally attached to them and did not forsake them. Their
fondness did not cease. They did not consider the nature of imper-   603b
manence or the impurity of foul exposure. With these anxieties
they became internally ill. With his eye of wisdom the Buddha
knew that their thoughts were disturbed and that their minds
were rampant with desire. They were unable to settle down their
thoughts and thus they could not be saved. The Buddha made one
of them go away, and transformed himself into that man. He entered the room [where the other man remained] and asked: "The
ideas we have in mind do not go away. We might both go and have
a look. When we see their appearances we shall know what they
are like. Yes, our vain imaginings are utterly tiresome and amount
to nothing." Both men left the dwelling and arrived in a village
with dissolute women. The Buddha magically created a prostitute

in the village. They both entered her dwelling and said to her: "We, men of the Path, have received the Buddha's prohibitory precept not to perform any sexual act. It is our intention to have a look at a woman's personal beauty. We shall pay the price, following the policy." Thereupon the transformed woman took off her necklaces and her perfumed clothes. She stood there naked and her offensive smelly part was difficult to approach. When the two men looked at her, they fully saw her foul exposure. The transformed ascetic then said to the other: "A woman's beauty just consists of cosmetics, perfumes, and flowers. She bathes and smears ointments. She wears clothes of different hues to cover her foul exposure. She vigorously applies fragrances and wants people to gaze at her. Just like a skin bag filled with manure, what is there desirable about her?" Thereupon the transformed monk spoke the stanzas:

> 16. Desire, I know your root! In my mind you are produced by thoughts. If I do not think of you, then you do not exist!

> 17. If the mind allows, then it becomes desire. Why necessarily just five desires! If one can swiftly destroy the five desires, he is a brave one.

> 18. Without desire and without fear one is undisturbed and without grief. When desire is removed and fetters are undone, he is someone out of the abyss for a long time.

After the Buddha had spoken the stanzas, he manifested his brilliant appearance. When the monk saw this, he was ashamed and repented of his wrongdoing. He fell prostrate and did obeisance to the Buddha, who again expounded the Doctrine to him. He was glad and gained understanding, and he attained arhatship. When the other man returned, he saw that his companion's expression was happier than usual. So he asked his companion why he was like that. The companion then gave an explanation according to the facts. The Buddha's great compassion had caused the rescue. Having received the World-honored One's mercy, he had been able to escape from every suffering. Thereupon the monk further spoke the stanza:

> 19. If day and night one thinks of desire and the mind wanders, not giving any thought to curbing it, one will then long for her foul exposure on seeing a woman. When one's imaginings are extinguished, one is free from sorrow.

When his companion, the monk, heard this stanza, he immediately started reflecting. He did away with his desire, extinguished his imaginings, and attained the eye of the Doctrine.

Chapter XXXIII

Nurturing by Gain

Once the Buddha led his disciples to the pure abode of Ghoṣila in the land of Kauśāmbī, and expounded the Doctrine to gods, men, spirits, and dragons. The king was called Udayana. He had a wife who practiced benevolence and was famous for her purity. He valued her principles and respected her privately. When he heard that the Buddha had come to make conversions, he made preparations for both to go to where the Buddha was. They did obeisance to the Buddha, withdrew, and sat down according to their regular rank. The Buddha explained to the king, his wife, and the ladies in waiting the nature of the following: impermanence, suffering, the void, why man is reborn, that what comes together must separate, that meeting with enmity is painful, that one is reborn in heaven because of one's merits, and that one enters the abyss because of one's evil. The king and his wife were happy and gained pious understanding. Each accepted the five precepts and became a man and wife with pure faith. They saluted the Buddha and withdrew, returning to the palace.

There once was a brahman called Māgandika who had a most lovely daughter unequaled in the society. When she was sixteen years old, no one could find fault with her. He offered a reward of a thousand taels over a period of ninety days to find that she was not an upright woman, [and if someone could] the money would be given away, but no one complied. As she attained womanhood, she should find someone to marry. He pondered on the possible person: "If there is anyone who is as upright as my daughter, I shall give him my daughter. I have heard about the monk Gautama of the Śākya clan. His appearance is golden and rare in the world.

191

I shall go and give this daughter in marriage to him." So he took her to the Buddha, did obeisance, and informed the Buddha: "My daughter's loveliness is unequaled in society. She has grown up and should marry, but there is no suitable companion in society. Your beauty, Gautama, may be considered as the equal of hers. That is why I have come with her from afar to make her your companion, World-honored One." The Buddha informed Māgandika: "Your daughter's beauty, sir, is considered good by her family, but my beauty is considered good by the Buddhas. My good appearance and beauty are in principle not the same. You, sir, praise the beauty of your daughter as truly good. She is like a painted vase filled with excrement. What is particularly fine about that? Her beauty is local, attached to the great villains of her eyes, ears, nose, mouth, and body. The beauty of an outward appearance is a great personal calamity. It destroys one's house and extinguishes one's family. It kills relatives and harms children. All this because of a woman's beauty! I am an ascetic. I stand alone, all by myself. Although I am afraid of real danger, how much less would I accept your disastrous and villainous offspring! Go away, sir! I do not

604a accept her." Thereupon the brahman became angry and left. He went to King Udayana, praised the attractiveness of his daughter and told the king: "By her looks this daughter should be your concubine. Because she is of age I present her to you now, O king." When the king saw her he was happy, and immediately accepted her. She respectfully agreed to be his second, subordinate wife. He conferred his official seal, gold and silver, and precious things on Māgandika, who respectfully agreed to be his councilor. When this woman obtained her rank, she was always jealous and her witchcraft misled the king. She spoke ill of the first wife, and not just once. But the king put her to shame, saying: "You allure me, but your words are insolent. The deportment of that person [i.e., the first wife] is honorable, and yet you speak ill of her." The thoughts of this woman were malicious as she still wanted to harm her. She kept on speaking ill, and the king was somewhat perplexed. Always scheming, she secretly waited for the time of fasting. Then she advised the king: "It would be proper to invite your esteemed wife to today's auspicious event." The king then issued a general summons for all to gather. His first wife kept her fast and she alone did not comply with the order. He repeated it and called her three more times, but she kept her fast and did not move. The king was in a great rage and sent someone to drag her out. He had her tied up in front of his palace and prepared to shoot her dead. But his wife was not afraid, as she wholeheartedly took refuge in the Buddha. The king himself shot at her, but the arrow returned to him. Another shot, and it returned at once. And so it was with several more arrows. The king had great fear by then. Untying her, he asked: "What artifice do you have that you bring this about?" His wife replied: "I just serve the Tathāgata. I have taken refuge in the Buddha, Dharma, and Sangha. In the morning I observe the penance of the Doctrine and I do not eat after noon. I observe the eight things, and I do not have ornaments near me. It must be that the World-honored One looked after me like that." The king said: "Excellent! How well said!" He immediately sent Māgandika away and the second wife was returned to her parents. He correctly established his first wife in the palace. The king, his first wife, the women of the palace, and the crown prince made preparations to leave, and along with their ministers they all went to where the Buddha was. They did obeisance, withdrew, sat down, and listened to the Doctrine with their hands folded. The king then gave the Buddha a complete explanation of the event according to the facts. The Buddha said to the great king: "A bewitching woman has eighty-four attitudes, but there are eight main attitudes, detested by the wise. Namely, which eight? One, jealousy; two, false anger; three, insulting; four, imprecation; five, repugnancy; six, greediness; seven, fondness for embellishment; eight, a poisonous mouth. These are the eight main attitudes." Thereupon the World-honored One spoke the stanzas:

1. Even a shower of the seven precious things will not satisfy one's desire. He who realizes that happiness is small [compared to] mountainous suffering is a wise one.

2. Even if there were celestial desires, a sage does not
covet but removes them. Happy to forsake affection, he is
a disciple of the Buddha.

The Buddha informed the great king: "The demerit and the merit
performed by man has each its own real nature. The retribution
reflected in each experience is ten-thousandfold, never equal. If
604b   one practices the six qualities and keeps the fast, the merits are
numerous. Praised by the Buddhas, one will finally be reborn in
the brahma heaven and the happiness based on merit will come
naturally." When the Buddha said this, the king, his wife, the
ladies in waiting, and great ministers all opened up their minds
and obtained the Path.

Chapter XXXIV

The Ascetic

Once the Buddha was in a pure abode in Śrāvastī, expounding the Doctrine to gods, dragons, spirits, the king, and his subjects. Then there was a young monk. At daybreak he donned his robe and with staff and bowl in hand, he went to a large village on his alms round. By the side of the main road, there was a vegetable garden cultivated by an official. At the edge of the garden he planted millet. In the outer grassy area of the garden, he had installed a net to discharge arrows. If an animal or thief were to disturb it, an arrow would be discharged upon touching the net, killing the intruder. A beautiful young girl guarded this garden alone. If someone wanted to go in, she called out from afar and showed the way to safely enter. Someone who did not know the way was sure to be killed by a discharged arrow. However, while this girl was on guard all by herself, she sang melancholy songs. Her voice was clear and bewitching. Of those who heard it, there was none who did not halt his chariot or horse. They turned around and, mincing their steps, they wanted to hurry to her, but they lingered about and did not go further. They were all under the spell of her voice. Then, when this monk had gone on his alms round, on his way back, he heard her singing. He inclined his ear and listened to her voice, and his five feelings were aroused. His thoughts were confused and his mind disturbed. He was seized by desire and could not forsake it. He imagined that this woman must surely be very beautiful. As he was thinking, he wanted to meet her, sit down, and start a conversation. So he turned around and walked toward her. Before he was halfway there, his mind was in a flurry. His hand let go of his staff, his robe fell from his shoulder, and he lost his alms bowl, but he did not really notice. The Buddha saw with his three penetrating insights that if this monk went a little further, he would be killed by an arrow. Through his merit he deserved to obtain the Path, although he was misled by foolishness and overwhelmed by the screen of desire. The Buddha had pity on his foolishness and wanted to save him. He changed himself into someone clad in white and went to his side. He reprimanded him with the stanzas:

> 1. If the practice of an ascetic means just following one's whims without any restraint, then with every step taken, one will get stuck deeper. He merely follows his [stray] thoughts.

> 2. He wears the *kāṣāya* over his shoulder, but he still performs evil and does not destroy it. When the evildoer dies, he falls into a woeful destination.

> 3. Cut off from the stream, ponder by yourself! Stop your [stray] thoughts and drive away desire! If one does not sever desire, a thought will accordingly run its course.

> 4. Do it! Do it! You must restrain yourself with force! When one has renounced home but is indolent, the mind is still tainted.

604c
> 5. He whose conduct is indolent must exert his will, not suspend it! If conduct is not clean or pure, how could it bring about the great treasures?

> 6. If one is not trained and hard to instruct, he is like a tree withered by the wind. A person is of his own making. Why not be zealous?

Having spoken these stanzas he returned to his own appearance. His primary and secondary marks were evident and his light illuminated heaven and earth. Anyone who saw it had his delusion cleared away and his confusion ended. They were all back in their element. When the monk saw the Buddha, his mind suddenly opened up, as when observing a light in darkness. He immediately fell prostrate and did obeisance to the Buddha. He kowtowed, repented his wrongdoing, confessed, and apologized to the Buddha. When he had deeply understood tranquility and insight, he attained arhatship and followed the Buddha back to the pure abode. The countless [people] who heard this all attained the eye of the Doctrine.

Chapter XXXV

The Brahman

Once, in the land of Ssu-ho-tieh, there were big mountains called Ssu-hsiu-che-t'o. In the mountains there were more than five hundred brahmans who excelled in the superknowledges. They said to each other: "What we have attained is exactly nirvana." Meanwhile, the Buddha had just appeared in the world to establish the Doctrine to open up the gate of immortality. The brahmans heard about it, but they did not go to meet him. They deserved to be saved, however, because of their previous merits. The Buddha went to them alone, without a companion. At the entrance of the road he sat down under a tree. As his mind concentrated in meditation (*samādhi*), light emitted from his body and illuminated the whole mountain. The whole mountain was ablaze as if it were on fire. The brahmans were frightened. They recited incantations over water and tried to extinguish it. They exhausted their divine powers and were unable to extinguish it. They felt strange and gave up, and then left the mountains following the road. In the distance they saw the World-honored One meditating under a tree, as if the sun had risen at the edge of the golden mountains. His primary and secondary marks were evident, just like the moon among the stars. They wondered what kind of spirit he was. They approached him and gazed at him. The Buddha bade them sit down, and asked them where they came from. The brahmans replied: "We are staying in these mountains, and we have long been practicing the Path, but at dawn a fire suddenly started, burning the trees in the mountains. We were frightened and left." The Buddha informed the brahmans: "This is the fire of merit. It does not harm anyone. It wants to extinguish your impurity, the fetter of delusion." The brahmans, masters and followers, turned their heads and said to each other: "Who is this man of the Path? Among the ninety-six kinds there never was this master." They said [to each other]: "We have heard that the son of King Śuddhodana, called Siddhārtha, was not happy with his majestic position and that he has gone forth in search of Buddhahood. Might he not be the one?" The disciples asked the masters to question the Buddha on whether the practices of the brahmans were correct or not. The masters and the followers all rose and said to the Buddha: "The scriptural doctrine of brahmans, called the four non-obstructions, including astronomy, geography, regnal rule, rules which govern the people, and the ninety-six kinds of magical arts, are the rules that should be practiced. Are these scriptural texts the way to nirvana? Please, O Buddha, explain and disclose what we have not yet heard!" The Buddha informed the brahmans: "Listen well and think about it! Countless eons of previous lives I have constantly been practicing these scriptures. Having attained the five superknowledges too, moving mountains and stopping currents, I still passed through countless cycles of birth and death. I neither attained nirvana nor did I hear of someone who had attained the Path. Such practices as yours cannot be those of brahmans." Thereupon the World-honored One sighed and spoke the stanzas:

605a

> 1. When, having crossed the stream, one is desireless like Brahmā and knows that the formations have ended, I call him a brahman.

> 2. When, because he does not have two [separate] doctrines, he is pure and has crossed the abyss and his fetters of desire are undone, I call him a brahman.

> 3. One is not called a brahman because one has matted hair. When one sincerely practices in accord with the Doctrine, he is pure and wise.

> 4. When one has adorned one's hair but has no wisdom, for what purpose is a simple coarse garment! When

inwardly one is not free from attachment, what is the gain in one's outward [show of] rejection!

5. When one has removed lust, hatred, delusion, conceit, and all evil, like a snake casting off its skin, I call him a brahman.

6. When one has relinquished worldly things and does not utter harsh words, and is mindful of the eightfold path, I call him a brahman.

7. When, having done away with affection, one has left home, become free from desire, and removed attachment to craving itself, I call him a brahman.

8. When one shuns the places where people gather, does not fall into a gathering of gods, and does not revert back to any gathering, I call him a brahman.

9. When one is knowledgeable concerning one's previous lives, where one has come from time and again, when one's cycles of birth and death have ended, when one understands the profundity of the Path, and one is as wise as the one who is silent (the *muni*), I call him a brahman.

After the Buddha had spoken the stanzas he informed the brahmans: "As for what you have practiced, you think that you 605b have already attained nirvana. Just like fish in shallow water, how could you have lasting happiness! It is actually missing in your lives!" When the brahmans heard his teaching, an inner joy arose in their five feelings. They knelt deeply and said to the Buddha that they wished to be his disciples. Their hair fell off naturally and they immediately became ascetics. Because they had previously conducted themselves in purity, they attained the Path and became arhats. The gods, dragons, and spirits of the mountains all attained the Path.

Chapter XXXVI

Nirvana

Once the Buddha was on Mount Gṛdhrakūṭa near the city of Rājagṛha, together with one thousand two hundred fifty monks. At that time the king of Magadha was called Ajātaśatru. Each of the one hundred countries he controlled had a name. Nearby there was a country called Vṛji. It did not obey the king's orders. Therefore, he wanted to attack it, and forthwith summoned his ministers. In the discussion he argued: "The people of Vṛji are extremely well off. They produce plenty of precious things but do not submit to me! Should we rather raise troops to attack them?" In the land there was a wise lord, the prime minister, called Varṣakāra, who replied: "Yes, indeed." The king said to Varṣakāra: "The Buddha is not far from here. With his three insights of a noble sage there is nothing he does not see clearly. Bring my words to where the Buddha is! Ask him the full details according to your sentiment and ability! If I want to attack them, will I gain a victory or not?" When the prime minister received the instruction, he had a wagon and horses prepared and went to the pure abode. When he arrived, he did obeisance to the Buddha, his head touching the ground. The Buddha bade him sit down and he took a seat. The Buddha asked the prime minister where he came from, and the minister replied: "The king sends me." He kowtowed at the Buddha's feet and asked how he was, whether he was taking his meals as usual. The Buddha then asked the lord: "Are the king, the people, and the subjects of his land all in peace?" The minister said that the sovereign of the land and the people were all receiving the Buddha's grace. He informed the Buddha: "The king feels dislike toward the country of Vṛji and wants to attack it. Can he, according to your noble opinion, O Buddha, gain a victory?" The Buddha informed the minister: "If the people of the country of Vṛji are carrying out seven rules, one cannot have victory over them. The king must think carefully! He must not initiate anything recklessly!" The minister then asked the Buddha what the seven rules were. The Buddha said: "The people of Vṛji frequently gather together to discuss the right Doctrine. While developing merit they guard themselves and take this to be their norm. This is namely the first [rule]. The people of the country of Vṛji, the ruler, and his ministers are in constant harmony. They are very loyal in their duties. Whether instructing or carrying out their duties, they do not offend anyone. This is namely the second [rule]. The people of Vṛji are involved in observing the Law. There is nothing they do not attend to, and they also do not dare commit any violation. Superior and inferior comply with the rules. This is namely the third [rule]. The people of Vṛji are courteous and respectful. Men and women are separate, but the old and young are together. They do not commit any breach of the rules of proper deportment. This is namely the fourth [rule]. The people of Vṛji piously care for their parents and are obedient to their elders. They receive instructions on the acceptance of the precepts and consider this to be a national rule. This is namely the fifth [rule]. The people of the country of Vṛji support heaven and are in harmony with the earth. They venerate the gods of the soil and grain. They respectfully comply with the four seasons, and do not neglect farming. This is namely the sixth [rule]. The people of the country of Vṛji honor the Path and respect virtue. In the land there are ascetics who have attained the Path and who are arhats. When someone has come from afar, they worship him and provide clothing, bedding, and medicine. This is namely the seventh [rule]. Now, when the lord of a country acts according to these seven rules, he cannot easily be endangered. Even if all the people in the world went to attack him, they could not gain a victory." The Buddha informed the minister: "If the people of Vṛji were to observe even

605c

a single rule, one still must not attack them. How much less when they observe all seven such rules!" Thereupon the World-honored One spoke the stanza:

> 1. An advantageous victory must not be relied on! Even if one wins, one shall suffer further yet. Strive for the winning Doctrine! Being victorious, nothing is really produced!

When Prime Minister Varṣakāra heard the stanza expounded by the Buddha, he immediately attained the Path. Young and old at the meeting all attained the path of the stream-enterer. The minister then rose from his seat and said to the Buddha: "The affairs of the state are very troublesome. I wish to return. Please excuse me." The Buddha said: "You may, but keep this event in mind." He then rose from his seat, did obeisance to the Buddha, and left. Upon his return he reported everything to the king, who then gave up his attack. He upheld the Buddha's majestic teaching and thereby transformed his nation. The people of Vṛji then came and obeyed his orders. Superiors and inferiors were respectful to one another and the land consequently prospered.

Chapter XXXVII

The Birth and Death Cycle

Once the Buddha was in the pure abode of the Jetavana in the land of Śrāvastī, widely expounding the wondrous Doctrine to gods and men and to the king and his high officials. There was an elderly brahman who was dwelling along the road and his wealth was immeasurable. He had a son who was twenty years of age and who had recently married, not yet fully seven days. Husband and wife respected each other and their words were in harmony. The wife said to her husband: "I would like to go to the rear garden to have a look and enjoy myself. Couldn't we go there?" It was the third month of spring when they went to the rear garden. There was a tall mango tree that was high and had beautiful blossoms. The wife wanted some flowers, but there was no one who could get them for her. The husband of course knew what was on his wife's mind, and so he wanted to comply with her wishes. He immediately climbed up the tree to fetch a flower. He wanted to get one more and yet another as he climbed the tree again and again. Finally he reached a small branch which snapped. He fell to the 606a ground, was injured badly, and died. The whole family, young and old, was in a frenzy as they ran to where the son was. Calling out to heaven they mourned but then stopped and came to their senses again. Kinsmen far and near came in countless numbers, and they were all very grieved. All who heard about it were heartbroken. All who had seen it were painfully distressed. His parents and wife blamed heaven and earth, thinking they had not protected him. They placed him in a coffin and covered him with his garments, giving him a burial according to the rules. When they returned home they wept and were unable to stop weeping. Thereupon the World-honored One was saddened by their foolishness. He went to ask how they were. When the household of the elder, young and old, saw the Buddha, they were moved and did obeisance. They stated their hardship in detail. The Buddha said to the elder: "Stop and listen to the Doctrine! Everything is impermanent and cannot possibly remain long! Having come into existence, one will die, and evil and merit will follow. As for this son, in three places one weeps for him. The distress may cease, but still it is hard to overcome. Whose son is it, after all? Who are his relatives?" Thereupon the World-honored One spoke the stanzas:

1. Life is like a fruit that ripens, always in fear that it might fall. Having come into being, all experience suffering. Who then can bring about immortality?

2. From the beginning one finds pleasure in desire. Because of lewdness one enters the shadow of the womb. Having received a form, life moves like lightning, flowing night and day and difficult to halt.

3. This body is a mortal thing, but the spirit is a formless entity. If life expires, it will be reborn, but evil and merit are not lost.

4. Beginning and end are not [limited to] one generation, but delusion remains longer as a result of desire. One creates and experiences one's own suffering and happiness. Although the body dies, the spirit does not perish.

When the elder heard the stanzas, he understood their meaning and forgot his sorrow. He knelt deeply and said to the Buddha: "What evil did this son commit in his previous life, that he met an untimely death in his wonderful life? Please explain the misdeed he committed previously!" The Buddha informed the elder: "Well, in the past there was a young child who played with bow and arrows among the divine trees. Nearby there were three other people.

When they saw a sparrow high on a tree, the young child wanted to shoot it down. The three people urged him on: 'If you can hit the sparrow, people will praise you as a hero.' The young child thought it was fine. He drew his bow and shot the sparrow which died instantly, falling to the ground. The three people all laughed. They joined him in their merriment and then each went his way. They passed through the cycle of birth and death for countless eons. They encountered each other wherever they existed and all met and experienced their evil. One of the three people had merit, however, and he is now in heaven. One is reborn in the sea and has transformed there into a dragon king. One is yourself now, O elder. This young child was previously reborn in heaven and was the son of a god. When his life ended he descended and was reborn as your son, O elder. He fell from the tree, and when his life ended he was immediately reborn in the sea as the son of the transformed dragon king. On the very day of his rebirth a transformed bird king with golden wings took him and ate him up. Now two are distressed and weep in three places, I would say. It is your son who shot the sparrow in the past but who died now. The sparrow of the past is the transformed bird king with golden wings. The three people who had joined him in their merriment are you now, O elder, the god, and the dragon, who have lost their child. Because the bird king with golden wings has eaten him, today they are distressed and weeping in three places, I would say. Because they joined him in their merriment the retribution of these three is to weep." Thereupon the World-honored One spoke the stanzas:

606b

> 5. The spirit creates the three realms and the five places, both wholesome and unwholesome. While one quietly proceeds, they arrive in silence. That which is born responds quickly [like an echo].

> 6. The essence of form, desire, and formlessness all depend on one's former conduct. Just as a seed accords with its former appearance [of a tree], retribution naturally follows one's [former] shadow.

When the Buddha had spoken the stanzas, he wanted to open up the mind of the elder. So he manifested his previous life with his power of the Path, fully showing the events in heaven and among the dragons. The elder's mind opened up and he rose with joy. He knelt deeply, folded his hands, and said to the Buddha: "I and the young and old wish to be your disciples, O Buddha, dedicating ourselves to the five precepts and becoming *upāsakas*." The Buddha then conferred the precepts, and once again expounded the Doctrine and the meaning of impermanence to them. Young and old were glad, and they all attained the path of the stream-enterer.

Chapter XXXVIII

The Advantage of the Path

Once there was a king who ruled according to the right Doctrine; and the people longed for a change. But he had no heir apparent and this was sad. When the Buddha came to his country, he went out to visit the Honored One. Listening to the scriptures, he was glad, and he immediately accepted the five precepts. He observed them respectfully with all his heart, but his only wish was to have a son. Night and day he was zealous, not lax during the three moments. He had a servant who was eleven years old and who constantly served him. The servant was faithful, trustful, served the Law, and did not lose the dignity of his demeanor. He was humble, forbearing, and zealous. With all his heart he applied himself to the recitation of scriptural stanzas. In timely fashion, he got up first to take care of incense burning. He was zealous in such a manner for several years without growing weary. All of a sudden he fell seriously ill and it resulted in his [untimely] death; but his spirit returned and became the king's son. He was reared to adulthood and at fifteen years of age he was established as the heir apparent. When the life of the king, his father, had ended, by way of inheritance he became the king. He was arrogant and licentious, lewd and lustful. Night and day he was indolent and he did not manage the affairs of the land. His officers of state gave up the court and the people suffered from calamity. The Buddha knew that this behavior was not in agreement with his office, and so he led his disciples to that country. When the king heard about the Buddha's arrival, he did exactly as the late king. He welcomed him with a large crowd, kowtowed to the ground, withdrew, and sat on the king's seat. The Buddha said to the king: "The officers, the people, the officials, and ministers, are they all their usual selves?" The king said: "As a young man I am unable to find tranquility yet. We have all received your favors with gratitude, O Buddha. In this land there is no one else." The Buddha said to the king: "Do you know now, O king, where you actually came from or what merit you have performed to obtain this royal position?" The king said: "I wonder. In my ignorance I do not understand. I do not know where I came from in the previous world." The Buddha said to the great king: "Actually one becomes a king through five things. Which are the five? One, through giving one becomes a king. [Then] all people offer with reverence palaces and halls, and one's wealth is without limit. Two, constructing temples, and worshiping the Buddha, Dharma, and Sangha with bedding and decorative hangings, through this one becomes king. One governs the country on one's imperial seat in the main hall. Three, personally revering the Honorable Things and all venerables, through this one becomes a king. All people do obeisance to him. Four, forbearance of the three [evils] of the body and the four of the mouth, and seeing that the mind is without its three evils, through these one becomes a king. All who see this are glad. Five, in learning one always strives for wisdom. Through this one becomes a king. When making decisions about the affairs of the land, all respectfully apply them. When one practices these five things, one will be a king in every existence." Then the World-honored One spoke the stanzas:

> 1. When one knows how to wait on his superiors, the ruler, his father, his teacher, and men of the Path; when he is trustful, moral, charitable, learned, and wise, he will finally be lucky and peaceful in his rebirth.

> 2. When one had merit in his previous life, he will be honored among men in the next existence. When one brings peace to the world with the Path and serves the Doctrine, all will follow him.

3. The king is the lord of his ministers and people. He always loves his subjects with compassion. He leads in accord with the precepts of the Doctrine, and he exemplifies the Doctrine, propitious or otherwise.

4. Dwelling in safety, he does not forget danger. As his thinking is clear, his merit gradually increases. As for merit's recompense, it does not matter whether one is revered or despised.

The Buddha said to the king: "At the time of your previous existence, O King, you were a servant of the great king. You faithfully served the Buddha and the Doctrine with purity. You served the Sangha with respect, your relatives with piety, and your lord with loyalty. You always were zealous and charitable with all your heart. You exhausted yourself physically and suffered without being indolent. It was thus that your merit followed you and you became the king's son, complementing the king's splendor. Now you are honorable, but you are, on the other hand, indolent. If you are a king, you must practice the five things. What are the five things? One, guiding all people, without being condescending or abusive. 607a Two, training the officers, and receiving and giving in timely fashion. Three, mindfulness to the development of one's actions, while the merits do not cease. Four, trust in the right admonitions of loyal ministers, and do not accept slandering words that will harm those in the right. Five, do not allow the mind to be negligent, covetous, and desirous for affection. If one practices these five things, one's fame will extend to the four seas, and prosperity will come naturally. If one forsakes these five things, no principle will work. When people are in straits, their thinking is confused. When officers are weary, their authority does not function. A spiritual being without any merit is of no help, and a self-satisfied being lacks the great principle. When loyal ministers do not dare to admonish, and their thoughts are heedless, the land is not managed. When ministers are evil, people become resentful. In such conditions you will lose your good name, and later you will have no merit." Thereupon the World-honored One further spoke the stanzas:

> 5. When one leads a society by practicing what is right and refrains from wrong, and one controls his thoughts and overcomes all evil, such a one is a righteous king.

> 6. When one's perception is proper and one bestows kindness, and one is compassionate and likes to benefit others, benefiting them with impartiality, all feel close to such a one.

When the Buddha had said this, the king was very glad. He rose and stood in front of the Buddha. He fell prostrate in obeisance, confessed, and apologized to the Buddha. He immediately accepted the five precepts. When the Buddha again expounded the Doctrine he attained the path of the stream-enterer.

Once the Buddha was in the land of Śrāvastī, in the pure abode of the Jetavana, expounding the unsurpassed great Doctrine to gods and men, to the king, high officials, and the four classes of disciples. In the south of the land of Śrāvastī there were deep mountains. A wild elephant often appeared there which had three colors: white, blue, and black. The king wanted to have a famous great fighting elephant. So he dispatched someone to catch it and bring it back to be tamed by an elephant master. Within three years the elephant could be mounted and ordered into battle. At that time there also was a divine elephant, brought forth by a dragon. Its body was as white as snow and its tail as red as cinnabar. The two tusks looked like they were gold colored. When the hunter saw this exceptionally fine elephant, he returned to inform the king that there was another big elephant of such an appearance and fit to be ridden by a great king. The king immediately called more than thirty elephant catchers and ordered them to catch this elephant. They all went to where the elephant was and set a snare to catch it, but the divine elephant knew what was on their minds. So it immediately came forward as if to fall into their trap.

When they all came and wanted to catch it, the elephant became angry and rashly kicked and jumped at them. Those nearby were killed and those further away fled, but the elephant did not give up its pursuit.

On the flanks of the mountain there were young men of the Path, full of vigor and daring. They had been applying themselves to the Path in the mountains for a very long time, but they had not yet attained a concentrated mind. When one of the men of the Path saw from a distance the elephant chasing after and killing people, he felt pity and wanted to rescue them, [being] full of confidence and brave. When the Buddha saw this from afar, he was afraid that this monk would be killed by the divine elephant. So he went to the elephant's side and emitted a great bright light. When the elephant saw the Buddha's light, its anger ceased and its wrath was dispelled. It did not chase and kill people any longer. When the monk saw the Buddha, he drew back and did obeisance to him. The Buddha then spoke the stanza to the monk:

> 7. Do not recklessly disturb a divine elephant! You will only bring suffering and calamities on yourself. Evil intentions mean one's death, and that one will never reach a wholesome place.

When the monk had heard the stanza, he immediately kowtowed, confessed, and apologized for his wrongdoing. He inwardly and deeply rebuked himself and really felt himself to be wrong. In front of the Buddha he immediately attained arhatship. The men who had been catching the elephant came to their senses again. Those who had fled returned and they all attained the Path.

Once the Buddha was on Mount Gṛdhrakūṭa in Rājagṛha. King Bimbisāra then had a high official who had committed an offense. He discharged him and moved him to the mountains in the south, a thousand *li* from his country. Moreover, nobody lived there and the five cereals did not grow. But when the high official arrived there, the spring water flowed in excess and the five cereals grew in abundance. Those who were suffering from hunger or cold in the countries in the four quarters all came to this mountain. Within a few years there were three or four thousand families. To those who came he gave arable land, so that they might provide for their livelihood. The three elders among them and the senior members deliberated among themselves: "A country without a ruler is like a body without a head." They went to where the high official was, and installed him as their king. The high official replied to the elders: "If you take me as your king, it should be in conformity with the rules of a king! High officials, left and right, and both civilian and military leaders, high and low, should visit my court! One should present women to fill my palace! The taxes, grain, and silk should be in accordance with the civil laws!" The elders of the land said: "Indeed! We accept your commands. They should be in conformity with the rules of a king!" So they established him as their king. They placed in offices ministers as well as civilian and military leaders, high and low. They incited the people to construct the city walls and build houses, a palace, and pavilions. But [in the process] the people were subjected to suffering, and they could not take it any more. They started to think, and began to plot against the king. [One day] villainous ministers and associates took the king out hunting. They led the king into a marshy wilderness thirty or forty *li* from the city with the intention of killing him. The king asked those around him: "Why would you want to kill me?" They replied: "The people were fond of you when they were prosperous and happy. They served you, O king, with reverence. But now the people are in distress and their thoughts are running rampant. Families are in ruin; they plot against the state." The king informed them: "Sirs, it is of your own making. It is not my doing. If you unjustly kill me, the spirits will know about this. Let me have one wish so that I shall have no animosity in dying!" So he made the wish: "When I first opened up the wasteland, I produced cereals and nourished the people. Those who came all made a living. Their prosperity and happiness were without limit. They themselves promoted me and established me as their

king. They did this in accordance with the policies of other countries. If you nevertheless kill me now, I go without any real crime   607c
against the people. Should I die, I wish to become a flesh-eating
devil (*rākṣasa*) and enter my old body again. I shall avenge this
grievance." Thereupon they strangled him, abandoned his corpse,
and left. After three days the king's spirit became a flesh-eating
devil and was in his old body again. He was called Āṭavaka. He
then rose, entered the palace, and sucked up the new king, the
ladies of his harem, and the villainous ministers around him. He
killed them all. The devil left the palace in anger, and wanted to
kill everyone. The three elders in the land tied themselves with a
straw rope and went to the flesh-eating devil to surrender volun-
tarily. "This was done by villainous ministers. The populace could
not have known this. We implore your leniency. We hope you will
return to govern the land!" The [former] king said: "I am a devil.
How could I devote myself to the people! I have to obtain human
flesh as nourishment. A devil is irritable by nature. He is wrathful
and does not consider what may be grievous." The three elders
said: "The land is yours, O king. Therefore it should be as before,
but the nourishment you need will be a different matter." The
elders of the land issued an order that the people should all draw
lots to determine the sequence in which the families should provide
an infant to serve as live food for the devil king. Among the three
or four thousand families there was just one household whose
members were the Buddha's disciples. They were zealous in their
home, and did not violate the five precepts. They drew the lots
with the rest of the people and [unluckily] obtained the first lot.
They happened to have an infant who would be the first to be fed to
the devil king. The intelligent ones, young and old, were sorrowful
and lamented. They went far away to Mount Gṛdhrakūṭa and did
obeisance to the Buddha. They repented their wrongdoings and
rebuked themselves. The Buddha saw their suffering with his eye
of the Path, and he spontaneously declared: "Because of this infant,
I shall save countless people." He then flew alone to the devil's
gate. He manifested his bright form which illuminated the palace.

When the devil saw the light, he suspected it might be some special person. He immediately went out and saw the Buddha. He became malicious, and wanted to spring forward and suck up the Buddha, but the light pierced his eyes. Shouldering a mountain and spitting fire, he changed everything to dust. Only when he became weary after a long while did he surrender. He invited the Buddha in to sit down, and he kowtowed to the ground. The Buddha expounded the scriptural texts to him, and after carefully listening to the Doctrine he accepted the five precepts and became an *upāsaka*. He sent an officer to expedite his meal, to take the child

608a and bring it to him. The whole family loudly cried, and followed the child. Those who looked on were countless, grieving for them as the officer carried the child in his arms, lifted this food, and placed it in front of the devil. The devil then took this child, lifted the food, and went in front of the Buddha. He knelt deeply and said to the Buddha: "I am different from the people of the land if I take the child as my food. I have now accepted your five precepts, O Buddha, and I do not have to eat this child any more. Please let me offer this child to you, O Buddha. I present him to you, O Buddha." So the Buddha accepted him, expounded the Doctrine, and made an incantation. The devil was glad and attained the path of the stream-enterer. The Buddha placed the child in his bowl and took him out through the palace gates. He returned him to his parents and informed them: "Raise the infant in good health! Do not be sad any longer!" Of all the people who saw the Buddha there was none who was not startled. They wondered what spirit it was. "What merit does this child have that he was rescued, him alone? The devil's food was taken away and returned to the parents." Thereupon the World-honored One spoke the stanzas among the great multitude:

> 8. The quality of the precepts can be depended on. Its meritorious reward will always follow. He who sees the Doctrine is most respected among men. He finally keeps himself far from the three evil predestinations.

9. When the precepts are heeded, one removes any fear.
Meritorious reward is most revered in the three worlds.
Demons, dragons, or a snake's poison cannot harm a
person who maintains the precepts.

When the Buddha had spoken the stanzas, countless people saw the Buddha's radiant appearance; and they knew that he was the most honorable one, beyond compare in the three worlds. They were all converted and became the Buddha's disciples. They were glad on hearing the stanzas and all attained the Path.

Once the Buddha was in the Deer Park in the land of Benares expounding the Doctrine to a countless multitude, to gods and men, dragons and demons, and kings and their subjects. The crown princes of large kingdoms and their attendants, and the eldest sons of the princes of smaller kingdoms, more than five hundred people, went to where the Buddha was. They did obeisance to the Buddha, withdrew, and sat aside listening to the Doctrine. The crown princes then said to the Buddha: "Your Path, O Buddha, is fine, wondrous, and difficult to reach! Has there from of old ever been a king, a crown prince, a high official, or the son of an elder who has forsaken officialdom, love, and happiness to become an ascetic?" The Buddha informed the crown princes: "Happiness and love in the societies of the world are like an illusion, a mirage, a dream, or an echo. They suddenly come and they suddenly go in such a way that one cannot long sustain them." He further said: "Kings and crown princes, because of three things one cannot obtain the Path! What three? One, one is arrogant and does not have the mindfulness to study the fine meaning of the Buddha's scriptures in order to save one's spirit. Two, one is covetous and not mindful of being charitable to the poor and distressed. The wealth accumulated by officials and military officers is not shared with the people so that only their capital increases. Three, one cannot forsake lust and desire for affection and reject the distress 608b of its prison-like confines in order to become an ascetic, extinguishing all hardships and developing one's person. Therefore whosoever is born a bodhisattva is regal, and removing these three things one attains Buddhahood. There are three more things. What three? One, study when young and lead the people to transform while governing the land so that they will practice the ten wholesome [actions]. Two, in middle age give away your possessions to the poor and lonely, while your officials and military officers are as happy as the people! Three, truly reckon with the nature of impermanence! Life does not last long. Go forth and become ascetics, extinguishing painful causal conditions, and be free from further cycles of birth and death! If you do not practice the three things, you simply will not obtain anything!"

Thereupon the World-honored One stated: "Once, in a previous world, I was a noble universal sovereign, called Emperor Nemi, ruling with the seven precious things. There were palaces and pools, lodges and theaters, and also officials, crown princes, their wives and ladies, elephants and horses, and kitchen servants, each eighty-four thousand strong. Nemi had a thousand sons who were brave and skillful. One of them was worth a thousand men. He flew through the air and traveled throughout the four seas. He was sovereign in his actions, and no one was higher than he was. His lifespan was eighty-four thousand years. He governed according to the Doctrine and did not do wrong to his people. The noble king then thought to himself: 'Man's life is short, impermanent, and hard to preserve. I should just perform acts of merit, and thereby seek the truth of the Path. Keeping in mind being constantly charitable toward the people in the world, I shall share my riches with the people. Having seeded my merits, I shall just go forth and become an ascetic. Having eliminated desire, I shall attain the extinction of suffering.' So the king ordered his barber: 'If you see that [any one of] my hairs is white, inform me!' After a very long period, tens of thousands of years, the barber informed the king: 'You have a white hair.' The king ordered him to pull it out and put it on the table. When the king saw the white hair he wept and decreed: 'The first messenger has suddenly come again. Now that my hair is white, I must go forth and become an ascetic to seek the natural Path.' He lifted the hair in his palms and spoke the stanza:

10. My hair on top of my body has grown white now, and I am depleted. A heavenly messenger has given me notice that the time is right for me to go forth!

He immediately summoned his officials and installed his crown prince on the royal throne. He became an ascetic and entered the mountains to develop the Path. When his life as a man ended, he was immediately reborn in the second heaven as the crown prince of Śakra, emperor of the gods. Thereafter [born again on earth], he governed the world, simply as a great king. He again ordered his barber: 'If you see that [any one of] my hairs is white, inform me!' After a very long period, the barber again informed him: 'You [have a] white hair.' The king ordered him to pull it out, held it in his hands, and spoke the [same] stanza:

11. My hair on top of my body has grown white now, and I am   608c
depleted. A heavenly messenger has given me notice that
the time is right for me to go forth!

He again summoned his officials and installed his crown prince on the royal throne. He immediately became an ascetic and entered the mountains to develop the Path. When his life as a man ended, he was further reborn in heaven as Śakra, the emperor of the gods. When the former Śakra, the emperor of the gods, ended his life as a god, he descended to a rebirth in the world. He became the crown prince of a noble king. These three noble kings again became father and son. High above they were emperors of the gods, down below they were noble lords, and in the middle they were crown princes, thirty-six times each, to end and yet to begin, for several thousands of tens of thousands of years. When I practiced these three things, I realized Buddhahood. The father in those times is myself now. The crown prince is the worthy Śāriputra. The king's grandson is the worthy Ānanda. Following one another, they were reborn, and in this process they became kings in order to transform the world. Therefore I am especially honored, and I am beyond compare in the three worlds." When the Buddha said this, the king and his crown prince and all the other crown princes were very glad. They accepted the Buddha's five precepts, became *upāsaka*s, and attained the path of the stream-enterer.

Chapter XXXIX

Good Fortune

Once the Buddha was on Mount Gṛdhrakūṭa in Rājagṛha, turning the wheel of the Doctrine of the three vehicles for gods and men and for dragons and demons. Then, south of the mountains, on the bank of the Ganges, there lived a *nirgrantha* (Jain) brahman. When he first appeared he was already aged, learned, and very wise. His forte was the five superknowledges with his clear knowledge of the past and present. He had five hundred disciples under his wing. He taught and trained them, and they were all versed in astronomy, geography, the constellations, and human nature. There was nothing they did not look into as they examined both the internal and the external nature of things. Fate, luck, prosperity, and appearances, they all understood and firmly knew them. Through the actions of a former Buddha, the brahman's disciples deserved to obtain the Path. They all went together to the bank of the river. They arranged their seats and started a discussion by asking themselves: "As to the actions of the peoples in various societies, what can we consider good fortune in the world? We disciples do not understand!" They went to their teacher, did obeisance, and with folded hands said: "We disciples have been studying for a long time. We know well what we have studied, but we have not heard what the countries consider to be good fortune." The *nirgrantha* informed them: "Splendid is your question! In Jambudvīpa there are sixteen great countries and eighty-four thousand small countries. Each country has its own good fortune, whether it is gold or silver, crystal, lapis lazuli, the divine bright-moon gem, elephants or horses, chariots, beautiful women, coral, shells, fine music, a phoenix or a peacock, the sun, the moon, the stars, a precious vase, the four classes [of disciples], a brahman, or a man of the Path. These are the signs of good fortune, held dear by the countries. If they see them, their esteem is immeasurable. These are the signs, the good fortunes, of countries." The disciples said: "Could there rather be another very special good fortune which is beneficial to oneself, by which one may finally be reborn in heaven?" The *nirgrantha* replied: "Since the time of former teachers there has never been anything that surpasses these. No book records anything superior." The disciples said: "Recently we heard that someone of the Śākya clan has gone forth to practice the Path. He sat upright for six years, subdued Māra [the tempter], and became a Buddha. His three penetrating insights are unhindered. Let us all go and test him, selecting [items] from his wide knowledge. How about it, O great teacher?" The teacher and his followers, more than five hundred disciples, went along the mountain roads to where the Buddha was. They did obeisance to the Buddha and took their positions as brahmans. They folded their hands, knelt deeply, and said to the World-honored One: "As for the good fortune in every country, such are what the people are fond of, but we wonder if there is still something else that excels these." The Buddha informed the brahmans: "What you, sirs, are discussing refers to worldly things. By following them you may know good fortune. By going against them you may know misfortune. They cannot save man's spirit and deliver him from suffering. The doctrine of good fortune, as I know it, is that if you practice properly, you will obtain merit and be forever free from the three worlds. You will bring about nirvana." Thereupon the World-honored One spoke the stanzas:

1. The Buddha is honored above any god. The Tathāgata always shows what is meaningful when there is a brahman, a man of the Path, who comes to ask what is good fortune.

2. The Buddha feels pity and expounds what is really important. Devout happiness is the true Doctrine. It is the utmost good fortune.

224

3. And if one does not follow god or man in the hope and quest for luck, and if one does not pray and sacrifice to the spirits, this is the utmost good fortune.

4. Friendship with a worthy, selection of a good companion, constant and foremost performance of merits, and acceptance of the truth with all one's being, this is the utmost good fortune.

5. If one does away with evil and follows what is wholesome, if one avoids liquor, knows moderation, and does not lust after female beauty, this is the utmost good fortune.

6. If one is learned and practices the precepts, if one zealously applies oneself to the rules, and if one develops oneself, free from any strife, this is the utmost good fortune.

7. If one is pious as a layman and filially serves one's parents, if one regulates one's family and cares for wife and child, and if one's conduct is not deficient, this is the utmost good fortune.

8. If one is not arrogant or conceited, if one knows satisfaction and remembers to be thankful, and if one recites the scriptures properly and in a timely fashion, this is the utmost good fortune.

9. If one often patiently accepts what one hears, and if one is happy to meet an ascetic and quickly heeds his every exposition, this is the utmost good fortune.

10. If one observes the fast and develops pure conduct, if one persists in meeting the wise and stays close to the sages, this is the utmost good fortune. 609b

11. If one practices the qualities of the Path through faith, if one corrects one's intentions and directs himself toward the removal of doubt, and if one wants to rid

himself of the three evil predestinations, this is the utmost good fortune.

12. If one practices liberality with an impartial mind, if one serves those who have attained the Path and respects gods and men, this is the utmost good fortune.

13. If one always wants to free himself from desire, delusion, and hatred, and if one is able to practice insight into the true Path, this is the utmost good fortune.

14. If one rejects envious efforts and can faithfully apply oneself to the development of the Path, and if one constantly resorts to matters that are of [meaningful] concern, this is the utmost good fortune.

15. If everything in the world is established with a great compassionate mind, and if this brings about benevolence and peace to all beings, this is the utmost good fortune.

16. When the wise dwell in the world and always practice behavior reflecting good fortune, and when they bring about the perfection of their wise insight, this is the utmost good fortune.

When the brahmans heard the Buddha's teaching, they were very happy. They immediately did obeisance at the Buddha's feet and took refuge in the Buddha, his Doctrine, and his Order. When the brahmans, teacher and disciples, heard the Buddha's exposition of the stanzas, they were glad and their minds opened up. They were very happy, came forward, and said to the Buddha: "Very wonderful, World-honored One! Extraordinary in the world! There is a reason why we were deluded and unable to gain insight yet. We hope, World-honored One, that you will have compassion and save us. We wish personally to take refuge in the Three Honorable Things of the Buddha's Doctrine. We need to become ascetics and long to behave as such from now on!" When the Buddha said: "Excellent! Welcome, monks!", they immediately became ascetics.

They internally reflected on *ānāpāna* (breathing in and out) and attained arhatship. The countless listeners all attained the eye of the Doctrine.

Glossary

arhat: A perfect being who has freed himself from the bonds of birth and death by eliminating all passions. The ideal of early Buddhists.

bodhisattva: A sage on the way to becoming a Buddha.

eight inopportune births: The eight births that prevent one from seeing a Buddha or hearing the Dharma are (1) birth in hell; (2) birth in the realm of hungry spirits; (3) birth in the realm of beasts; (4) birth in the heaven of long life, where aspiration to enter the Buddhist Path does not arise; (5) birth in a remote land—in one of the heavens of the realms of form and formlessness or in Uttarakuru, one of the four continents in Buddhist cosmology—where sentient beings are absorbed in pleasures and do not seek the Dharma; (6) being born blind, deaf, or mute; (7) being knowledgeable about the world and eloquent; and (8) being born in a period before or after the Buddha's appearance in the world.

eight prohibitions: (1) Not to kill, (2) not to steal, (3) not to engage in sexual acts, (4) not to lie, (5) not to drink liquor, (6) not to use high or broad beds, (7) not to put perfumes or oils on the body nor to sing or dance, and (8) to eat only at designated times.

eightfold right path. *See* four noble truths.

emptiness: The quality that all things have of being devoid of any independent, real existence and existing only in dependence on everything else.

five aggregates: The five mental and physical factors that make up the nominal person, namely form, feeling, perception, impulse, and consciousness. What we call a "person" or "being" is simply these five factors; there is no self, person, soul, being, etc.

five precepts: The five precepts for Buddhist laypeople—(1) Not to kill, (2) not to steal, (3) not to commit adultery, (4) not to lie, and (5) not to use intoxicants.

four noble truths: (1) Life is suffering; (2) our attachments are the cause of suffering; (3) all suffering can be ended; (4) the way to end suffering is by following the Buddha's eightfold right path (i.e., right view, right thought, right speech, right action, right livelihood, right effort, right mindfulness, and right concentration).

nāga: A serpent.

non-returner: One who will never again return to or be reborn in this world of desires.

pratyekabuddha: A sage who attains enlightenment by observing the principles of causation and dependent arising by himself. He attains emancipation without the guidance of a teacher, and he intends neither to guide others nor to expound the teaching to others.

rākṣasa: A flesh-eating demon.

samādhi: A mental state of concentration and focusing of thought on one object. Also called meditation.

six realms of existence: (1) The realm of the gods, (2) the realm of humans, (3) the realm of fighting demons, (4) the realm of animals, (5) the realm of hungry ghosts, and (6) hell. All beings transmigrate through these realms in the cycle of birth and death in accordance with their karma.

stream-enterer: One who has entered the stream of the undefiled Noble Path and is on the way to enlightenment.

three woeful destinations: The three evil realms in which sentient beings transmigrate as retribution for evil deeds, namely, (1) hell, (2) the realm of hungry ghosts, and (3) the realm of animals.

triple refuge: The Buddha, the Dharma (the Buddha's teachings), and the Sangha (the community of his followers).

Bibliography

Beal, Samuel, trans. *Dhammapada with Accompanying Narratives*. Translated from the Chinese. 3rd ed. Varanasi: Indological Book House, 1971.

Dhammajati, Kuala Lumpur, trans. *The Chinese Version of Dharmapada = Fa chü ching chih Ying i chi yen chiu*. Colombo(?): Postgraduate Institute of Pali and Buddhist Studies, University of Kelaniya, c1995.

Lawrence, William Fawcett. *The Essence of Chinese Buddhism in the Earliest Chinese Dhammapada (c. 224 A.D.): A Blending of Buddhist, Confucian, and Taoist Teachings, Edited and Translated into English for the First Time with the Help of Buddhist Scholars in Japan*. San Marcos, CA: Fawcett, 1968.

Index

A

Ajātaśatru, King 143, 144, 145, 203

Āmrayaṣṭikā (pure abode) 171

anāgāmin. See non-returner

Ānanda (disciple of the Buddha) 10, 54, 68, 69, 75, 77, 134, 144, 145, 221

ānāpāna (breathing exercise) 20, 102, 227

Anāthapiṇḍada Grove 11, 18, 79, 111, 167

anger 7, 135, 143, 193, 215, 217

arhat(s) 10, 11, 13, 21, 29, 54, 60, 91, 93, 95, 103, 143, 144, 145, 201, 204

arhatship 18, 40, 75, 86, 89, 92, 95, 97, 100, 102, 111, 114, 116, 119, 123, 131, 134, 137, 141, 149, 153, 158, 163, 179, 184, 188, 197, 215

ascetic(s) 12, 18, 25, 26, 29, 41, 42, 43, 61, 62, 65, 66, 85, 86, 92, 96, 102, 104, 105, 109, 116, 121, 133, 134, 149, 151, 152, 156, 158, 161, 162, 165, 171, 172, 177, 178, 181, 182, 188, 192, 195, 196, 219, 220, 221, 225

Aśraddha (minister) 56

ass 7

Āṭavaka (demon) 217

Atibalavīryaparākrama (monk) 136

attachment 93, 201

Aṭṭhakathā (text) 1, 2

B

Bamboo Garden (*see also* Veṇuvana) 9, 10, 13, 134

bandit(s) 31, 32, 167, 187

barber 220, 221

Benares (city/region) 39, 81, 127, 128, 219

bhikṣuṇī. See nun

bhikṣu. See monk

Bimbisāra, King 41, 47, 51, 52, 215

birth(s) (*see also* rebirth) 14, 38, 62, 75, 86, 106

    eight inopportune 49

birth and death (cycle) 15, 19, 36, 46, 58, 59, 65, 74, 86, 88, 110, 128, 130, 135, 141, 157, 158, 161, 173, 175, 178, 183, 186, 200, 201, 207, 209, 220

boatman 84, 85, 86

bodhisattva(s) 67, 153, 220

Bodhi Tree 127

bow 25, 26, 32, 61, 83, 84, 208, 209

bow-makers 85, 86

Brahmā (god) 129, 145, 200

Brahmadeva (god) 67, 68

brahman(s) 11, 13, 14, 27, 28, 47, 49, 58, 59, 67, 77, 78, 79, 83, 85, 86, 97, 98, 100, 103, 104, 105, 111, 112, 113, 114, 115, 116, 117, 118, 123, 124, 125, 126, 127, 128, 129, 130, 131, 151, 155, 156, 157, 158, 165, 181, 191, 192, 199, 200, 201, 207, 223, 224, 226

Buddhaghosa (Buddhist teacher) 1, 2

A List of the Volumes of
the BDK English Tripiṭaka
(First Series)

Abbreviations

Ch.:	Chinese
Skt.:	Sanskrit
Jp.:	Japanese
Eng.:	Published title
T.:	Taishō Tripiṭaka

Vol. No.	Title		T. No.
1, 2	*Ch.*	Ch'ang-a-han-ching （長阿含經）	1
	Skt.	Dīrghāgama	
3–8	*Ch.*	Chung-a-han-ching （中阿含經）	26
	Skt.	Madhyamāgama	
9-I	*Ch.*	Ta-ch'eng-pên-shêng-hsin-ti-kuan-ching （大乘本生心地觀經）	159
9-II	*Ch.*	Fo-so-hsing-tsan （佛所行讚）	192
	Skt.	Buddhacarita	
10-I	*Ch.*	Tsa-pao-ts'ang-ching （雜寶藏經）	203
	Eng.	The Storehouse of Sundry Valuables	
10-II	*Ch.*	Fa-chü-p'i-yü-ching （法句譬喻經）	211
	Eng.	The Scriptural Text: Verses of the Doctrine, with Parables	
11-I	*Ch.*	Hsiao-p'in-pan-jo-po-lo-mi-ching （小品般若波羅蜜經）	227
	Skt.	Aṣṭasāhasrikā-prajñāpāramitā-sūtra	
11-II	*Ch.*	Chin-kang-pan-jo-po-lo-mi-ching （金剛般若波羅蜜經）	235
	Skt.	Vajracchedikā-prajñāpāramitā-sūtra	

Vol. No.		Title	*T*. No.
46-I	*Ch.*	Miao-fa-lien-hua-ching-yu-po-t'i-shê	1519
		（妙法蓮華經憂波提舍）	
	Skt.	Saddharmapuṇḍarīka-upadeśa	
46-II	*Ch.*	Fo-ti-ching-lun （佛地經論）	1530
	Skt.	Buddhabhūmisūtra-śāstra (?)	
46-III	*Ch.*	Shê-ta-ch'eng-lun（攝大乘論）	1593
	Skt.	Mahāyānasaṃgraha	
	Eng.	The Summary of the Great Vehicle	
47	*Ch.*	Shih-chu-p'i-p'o-sha-lun （十住毘婆沙論）	1521
	Skt.	Daśabhūmika-vibhāṣā (?)	
48, 49	*Ch.*	A-p'i-ta-mo-chü-shê-lun （阿毘達磨俱舍論）	1558
	Skt.	Abhidharmakośa-bhāṣya	
50–59	*Ch.*	Yü-ch'ieh-shih-ti-lun （瑜伽師地論）	1579
	Skt.	Yogācārabhūmi	
60-I	*Ch.*	Ch'êng-wei-shih-lun （成唯識論）	1585
	Eng.	Demonstration of Consciousness Only	
		(In Three Texts on Consciousness Only)	
60-II	*Ch.*	Wei-shih-san-shih-lun-sung （唯識三十論頌）	1586
	Skt.	Triṃśikā	
	Eng.	The Thirty Verses on Consciousness Only	
		(In Three Texts on Consciousness Only)	
60-III	*Ch.*	Wei-shih-êrh-shih-lun （唯識二十論）	1590
	Skt.	Viṃśatikā	
	Eng.	The Treatise in Twenty Verses on Consciousness Only	
		(In Three Texts on Consciousness Only)	
61-I	*Ch.*	Chung-lun （中論）	1564
	Skt.	Madhyamaka-śāstra	
61-II	*Ch.*	Pien-chung-pien-lun （辯中邊論）	1600
	Skt.	Madhyāntavibhāga	
61-III	*Ch.*	Ta-ch'eng-ch'êng-yeh-lun （大乘成業論）	1609
	Skt.	Karmasiddhiprakaraṇa	
61-IV	*Ch.*	Yin-ming-ju-chêng-li-lun （因明入正理論）	1630
	Skt.	Nyāyapraveśa	

Vol. No.		Title	T. No.
61-V	*Ch.*	Chin-kang-chên-lun （金剛針論）	1642
	Skt.	Vajrasūcī	
61-VI	*Ch.*	Chang-so-chih-lun （彰所知論）	1645
62	*Ch.*	Ta-ch'eng-chuang-yen-ching-lun （大乘莊嚴經論）	1604
	Skt.	Mahāyānasūtrālaṃkāra	
63-I	*Ch.*	Chiu-ching-i-ch'eng-pao-hsing-lun	1611
		（究竟一乘寶性論）	
	Skt.	Ratnagotravibhāgamahāyānottaratantra-śāstra	
63-II	*Ch.*	P'u-t'i-hsing-ching （菩提行經）	1662
	Skt.	Bodhicaryāvatāra	
63-III	*Ch.*	Chin-kang-ting-yü-ch'ieh-chung-fa-a-nou-to-	1665
		lo-san-miao-san-p'u-t'i-hsin-lun	
		（金剛頂瑜伽中發阿耨多羅三藐三菩提心論）	
63-IV	*Ch.*	Ta-ch'eng-ch'i-hsin-lun （大乘起信論）	1666
	Skt.	Mahāyānaśraddhotpāda-śāstra (?)	
63-V	*Ch.*	Na-hsien-pi-ch'iu-ching （那先比丘經）	1670
	Pāli	Milindapañhā	
64	*Ch.*	Ta-ch'eng-chi-p'u-sa-hsüeh-lun （大乘集菩薩學論）	1636
	Skt.	Śikṣāsamuccaya	
65	*Ch.*	Shih-mo-ho-yen-lun （釋摩訶衍論）	1688
66-I	*Ch.*	Pan-jo-po-lo-mi-to-hsin-ching-yu-tsan	1710
		（般若波羅蜜多心經幽賛）	
66-II	*Ch.*	Kuan-wu-liang-shou-fo-ching-shu	1753
		（觀無量壽佛經疏）	
66-III	*Ch.*	San-lun-hsüan-i （三論玄義）	1852
66-IV	*Ch.*	Chao-lun （肇論）	1858
67, 68	*Ch.*	Miao-fa-lien-hua-ching-hsüan-i	1716
		（妙法蓮華經玄義）	
69	*Ch.*	Ta-ch'eng-hsüan-lun （大乘玄論）	1853

Vol. No.		Title	T. No.
70-I	*Ch.*	Hua-yen-i-ch'eng-chiao-i-fên-ch'i-chang （華嚴一乘教義分齊章）	1866
70-II	*Ch.*	Yüan-jên-lun （原人論）	1886
70-III	*Ch.*	Hsiu-hsi-chih-kuan-tso-ch'an-fa-yao （修習止觀坐禪法要）	1915
70-IV	*Ch.*	T'ien-t'ai-ssŭ-chiao-i （天台四教儀）	1931
71, 72	*Ch.*	Mo-ho-chih-kuan （摩訶止觀）	1911
73-I	*Ch.*	Kuo-ch'ing-pai-lu （國清百録）	1934
73-II	*Ch.*	Liu-tsu-ta-shih-fa-pao-t'an-ching （六祖大師法寶壇經）	2008
73-III	*Ch.*	Huang-po-shan-tuan-chi-ch'an-shih-ch'uan- hsin-fa-yao （黃檗山斷際禪師傳心法要）	2012A
73-IV	*Ch.*	Yung-chia-chêng-tao-ko （永嘉證道歌）	2014
74-I	*Ch.* *Eng.*	Chên-chou-lin-chi-hui-chao-ch'an-shih-wu-lu （鎮州臨濟慧照禪師語録） The Recorded Sayings of Linji (In Three Chan Classics)	1985
74-II	*Ch.* *Eng.*	Wu-mên-kuan （無門關） Wumen's Gate (In Three Chan Classics)	2005
74-III	*Ch.* *Eng.*	Hsin-hsin-ming （信心銘） The Faith-Mind Maxim (In Three Chan Classics)	2010
74-IV	*Ch.*	Ch'ih-hsiu-pai-chang-ch'ing-kuei （勅修百丈清規）	2025
75	*Ch.* *Eng.*	Fo-kuo-yüan-wu-ch'an-shih-pi-yen-lu （佛果圜悟禪師碧巖録） The Blue Cliff Record	2003
76-I	*Ch.* *Skt.*	I-pu-tsung-lun-lun （異部宗輪論） Samayabhedoparacanacakra	2031
76-II	*Ch.* *Skt.* *Eng.*	A-yü-wang-ching （阿育王經） Aśokarāja-sūtra (?) The Biographical Scripture of King Aśoka	2043

Vol. No.		Title	T. No.
76-III	*Ch*.	Ma-ming-p'u-sa-ch'uan （馬鳴菩薩傳）	2046
76-IV	*Ch*.	Lung-shu-p'u-sa-ch'uan （龍樹菩薩傳）	2047
76-V	*Ch*.	P'o-sou-p'an-tou-fa-shih-ch'uan（婆藪槃豆法師傳）	2049
76-VI	*Ch*.	Pi-ch'iu-ni-ch'uan （比丘尼傳）	2063
76-VII	*Ch*.	Kao-sêng-fa-hsien-ch'uan （高僧法顯傳）	2085
76-VIII	*Ch*.	Yu-fang-chi-ch'ao: T'ang-ta-ho-shang-tung-chêng-ch'uan（遊方記抄: 唐大和上東征傳）	2089-(7)
77	*Ch*.	Ta-t'ang-ta-tz'ŭ-ên-ssŭ-san-ts'ang-fa-shih-ch'uan （大唐大慈恩寺三藏法師傳）	2053
	Eng.	A Biography of the Tripiṭaka Master of the Great Ci'en Monastery of the Great Tang Dynasty	
78	*Ch*.	Kao-sêng-ch'uan （高僧傳）	2059
79	*Ch*.	Ta-t'ang-hsi-yü-chi （大唐西域記）	2087
	Eng.	The Great Tang Dynasty Record of the Western Regions	
80	*Ch*.	Hung-ming-chi （弘明集）	2102
81–92	*Ch*.	Fa-yüan-chu-lin （法苑珠林）	2122
93-I	*Ch*.	Nan-hai-chi-kuei-nei-fa-ch'uan（南海寄歸內法傳）	2125
93-II	*Ch*.	Fan-yü-tsa-ming （梵語雜名）	2135
94-I	*Jp*.	Shō-man-gyō-gi-sho （勝鬘經義疏）	2185
94-II	*Jp*.	Yui-ma-kyō-gi-sho （維摩經義疏）	2186
95	*Jp*.	Hok-ke-gi-sho （法華義疏）	2187
96-I	*Jp*.	Han-nya-shin-gyō-hi-ken （般若心經秘鍵）	2203
96-II	*Jp*.	Dai-jō-hos-sō-ken-jin-shō （大乘法相研神章）	2309
96-III	*Jp*.	Kan-jin-kaku-mu-shō （觀心覺夢鈔）	2312

Vol. No.		Title	T. No.
97-I	*Jp.*	Ris-shū-kō-yō （律宗綱要）	2348
	Eng.	The Essentials of the Vinaya Tradition	
97-II	*Jp.*	Ten-dai-hok-ke-shū-gi-shū （天台法華宗義集）	2366
	Eng.	The Collected Teachings of the Tendai Lotus School	
97-III	*Jp.*	Ken-kai-ron （顯戒論）	2376
97-IV	*Jp.*	San-ge-gaku-shō-shiki （山家學生式）	2377
98-I	*Jp.*	Hi-zō-hō-yaku （秘藏寶鑰）	2426
98-II	*Jp.*	Ben-ken-mitsu-ni-kyō-ron （辨顯密二教論）	2427
98-III	*Jp.*	Soku-shin-jō-butsu-gi （即身成佛義）	2428
98-IV	*Jp.*	Shō-ji-jis-sō-gi （聲字實相義）	2429
98-V	*Jp.*	Un-ji-gi （吽字義）	2430
98-VI	*Jp.*	Go-rin-ku-ji-myō-hi-mitsu-shaku （五輪九字明秘密釋）	2514
98-VII	*Jp.*	Mitsu-gon-in-hotsu-ro-san-ge-mon （密嚴院發露懺悔文）	2527
98-VIII	*Jp.*	Kō-zen-go-koku-ron （興禪護國論）	2543
98-IX	*Jp.*	Fu-kan-za-zen-gi （普勸坐禪儀）	2580
99–103	*Jp.*	Shō-bō-gen-zō （正法眼藏）	2582
104-I	*Jp.*	Za-zen-yō-jin-ki （坐禪用心記）	2586
104-II	*Jp.*	Sen-chaku-hon-gan-nen-butsu-shū （選擇本願念佛集）	2608
	Eng.	Senchaku Hongan Nembutsu Shū	
104-III	*Jp.*	Ris-shō-an-koku-ron （立正安國論）	2688
104-IV	*Jp.*	Kai-moku-shō （開目抄）	2689
104-V	*Jp.*	Kan-jin-hon-zon-shō （觀心本尊抄）	2692
104-VI	*Ch.*	Fu-mu-ên-chung-ching （父母恩重經）	2887

Vol. No.		Title	T. No.
105-I	*Jp.*	Ken-jō-do-shin-jitsu-kyō-gyō-shō-mon-rui （顯淨土眞實教行証文類）	2646
105-II	*Jp.*	Tan-ni-shō （歎異抄）	2661
	Eng.	Tannishō: Passages Deploring Deviations of Faith	
106-I	*Jp.*	Ren-nyo-shō-nin-o-fumi （蓮如上人御文）	2668
	Eng.	Rennyo Shōnin Ofumi: The Letters of Rennyo	
106-II	*Jp.*	Ō-jō-yō-shū （往生要集）	2682
107-I	*Jp.*	Has-shū-kō-yō （八宗綱要）	蔵外
	Eng.	The Essentials of the Eight Traditions	
107-II	*Jp.*	San-gō-shī-ki （三教指帰）	蔵外
107-III	*Jp.*	Map-pō-tō-myō-ki （末法燈明記）	蔵外
	Eng.	The Candle of the Latter Dharma	
107-IV	*Jp.*	Jū-shichi-jō-ken-pō （十七條憲法）	蔵外